Middlesex Vol I
Edited by Sarah Marshall

 Young**Writers**

First published in Great Britain in 2005 by:
Young Writers
Remus House
Coltsfoot Drive
Peterborough
PE2 9JX
Telephone: 01733 890066
Website: www.youngwriters.co.uk

SB ISBN 1 84602 125 1

Foreword

Young Writers was established in 1991 and has been passionately devoted to the promotion of reading and writing in children and young adults ever since. The quest continues today. Young Writers remains as committed to the fostering of burgeoning poetic and literary talent as ever.

This year's Young Writers competition has proven as vibrant and dynamic as ever and we are delighted to present a showcase of the best poetry from across the UK. Each poem has been carefully selected from a wealth of *Playground Poets* entries before ultimately being published in this, our thirteenth primary school poetry series.

Once again, we have been supremely impressed by the overall high quality of the entries we have received. The imagination, energy and creativity which has gone into each young writer's entry made choosing the best poems a challenging and often difficult but ultimately hugely rewarding task - the general high standard of the work submitted amply vindicating this opportunity to bring their poetry to a larger appreciative audience.

We sincerely hope you are pleased with our final selection and that you will enjoy *Playground Poets Middlesex Vol I* for many years to come.

Contents

Alpha Preparatory School

Jack Hayes (8) 1

Imogen Drummond (7) 1

Simran Sagoo Dass (9) 2

Yasmin Fernandes (7) 2

Jeevan Singh (8) 3

Faheem Bashir (7) 3

Nathalie Kelly (9) 4

Abhijay Sood (7) 4

Nikhil Patel (9) 5

Bhavini M Sheth (7) 5

Samantha Carmichael (9) 6

Shiv Patel (7) 6

Zakariya Sheikh (8) 7

Eisha Patel (8) 7

Rachel Still (9) 8

Prabhleen Oberoi (7) 8

Kayetan Shrimanker (8) 9

Dilankumar Patel (7) 9

Shria Patel (8) 10

Gurpreet Mudhar (7) 10

Samee Deen (9) 11

Rohit Amlani (7) 11

Saday Lakhani (9) 12

Darshana Patel (7) 12

Rishi Gillman-Smith (9) 13

Cameron Sammakieh (7) 13

Anjli Patel (9) 14

Shaquille McCoy-Neil (7) 14

Sahana Chrishanthan (8) 15

Shekinah Simpson (7) 15

Lanre Ige (8) 16

Devang Shah (8) 16

Ravi Achan (8) 17

Rishi Gandhi (7) 17

Shenaya Nadesan (8) 18

Sachin Gandhi (8) 18

Kayleigh Simion (8) 19

Coston Primary School

Elyar Afshari (9)	19
Karen Abousaleh (10)	20
Aursh Patel (7)	20
Kajal Tutt (7)	21
Lorrianne Joseph (8)	21
Tavneet Flora (8)	21
Rakim Sajero (7)	22
Saif Elcafagi (8)	22
Charlotte Nixon (8)	22
Zaynah Rasheed (9)	23
Lulu Landers (8)	23
Emily Maguire (10)	23
Magdalena Zamojska (8)	24
Nathan Lo (10)	24
Amar Tateri (10)	24
Jessica Baradaran (10)	25
Vivek Bhatti (11)	25
Nadia Mills (11)	25
Ameer Hussain (8)	26
Henry Matthews (8)	26
Gaurav Prinja (8)	26
Sophia Anderson Ekwere (10)	27
Narinder Thethi (10)	27
Hummera Khan (10)	27
Harjot Kaur Grewal (11)	28
Rochae Cook-Anderson (11)	28
Luke Lasenby (10)	28
Nida Shah (10)	29
Imran Malik (9)	29
June Digby (9)	30
Mohamed Ahmed (8)	30
Huma Shaikh (8)	30
Jennifer Rose (9)	31
Bavita Tateri (8)	31
Jordan Luckett (10)	31
Charlie Kelleher-Gibbons (8)	32
Tillan Kailarajan (8)	32
Melissa Neocleous (10)	32
Dania Al-Khangi (11)	33
Luke Bishop (10)	33

Marina Shurakova (10)   33
Laurence Azadbakht (10)   34
Jay-Jay Parke-Jude (11)   34
Jay Strutton (10)   34
Ben House (11)   35
Nadia El-Kandil (9)   35
Mark Augustine (11)   36
Ivana Joseph (11)   36
Sabah El-Safi (11)   36
Kalelah Benjamin (7)   37
L'Amour Sajero (8)   37
Jounee Rodney (7)   37
Paul Chinkwende (8)   37
Mickel Kruythoff (8)   38
Christopher Redmond (7)   38
Khaleel Begg (7)   38
Harseen Khailany (7)   39
Tevin Williamson (10)   39
Mariam Polad (9)   39
Sammy Kaur Sidhu (9)   40
Amy Nixon (10)   40
Mustafa Mohammed (10)   40
Owen Kelley Patterson (9)   41
Anthony Francis (10)   41
Farhan Khan (7)   41
Joel Hamilton (10)   42
Zeshan Khalid (10)   42
Olivia McLeod (7)   42
Sam House (6)   43
Taran Sidhu (6)   43
Ricky Heavans (7)   43
Devna Patel (7)   44
Kiah Sylvan (7)   44
Diane-Louie Baker-Dee (6)   44
Sulaymaan Dar (6)   45
Rachel Duke (7)   45
Xena Hawkins (6)   45
Parth Patel (7)   45
Sadia Shafi (7)   46
Sarah Glenton (7)   46
Renee Francis (7)   46

Joshua Gaunt (6)   46
Dannieller Lemiare (7)   47

Dormers Wells Junior School
Sinthusan Gunaratnam (10)   47
Renu Shoor (9)   48
Muhammad Hasan (10)   48
Priya Sharma (9)   49
Akshay Patel (10)   49
Puneet Bhachu (10)   50
Vickram Singh (9)   50
Amardeep Dosanjh (9)   51
Hasib Mahmoud (8)   51
Jaathushan Ganesapathy (10)   52
Ikram Musse (8)   52
Qasim Farid (10)   53
Roop Bhinder (9)   53
Abdi Adnan (10)   54
Aamina Deen (9)   54
Shangavee Sivaselvaraja (10)   55
Bijal Patel (9)   56
Simrandeep Gill (9)   56
Manpreet Kaur Rajbans (8)   57
Sara Haider (10)   57
Zahra Deen (8)   58
Devesh Sharma (9)   58
Huda Hassan (10)   59
Maryam Naz (9)   59
Harvind Khosa (9)   60
Saleh Zaheer (8)   61
Lincy Fernandez (9)   61
Manish Pandey (8)   62

Echelford Primary School
Daniela Bertoglio, Danielle Fenwick, Madeleine Dave,
    Emma Burrows & Melissa Soden (10)   62
Katherine Church (10)   63
Alexandra Dennis (8)   64
Charley Jagger (9)   64
Thomas Wyse Jackson (11)   65
Eloise Hutchins (9)   65

Alice Dowdeswell (8)	66
Lucy Butler (8)	66
Sophie Lock (8)	67
Natalie Butler (9)	67
Lucy Hickman (9)	68
Tom Hunt (8)	68
Adam See (10)	69
Sean McCarthy (9)	69
Emma Stubbs (9)	70
Daniel Nielsen (8)	70
Jemma Pearce (8)	71
Georgia Phillips (9)	71
Emily Brambleby (10)	72
Danny Woods (10)	73
Thomas Giles (10)	74
Rory Thomas (9)	74
Dean Horsburgh (10)	75
Becky Ware (10)	76
Hayleigh Whiteside (10)	77
Megan Lewis (10)	78
Jonathan Aspin (10)	79

Edward Pauling Primary School

Safia Ballout (9)	80
Elsie Constantinides (8)	80
Samantha Cooley (8)	81
Jake Cumming (8)	81
Talal Mussa (9)	82
Naomi Lloyd-Barling (9)	82
Max Brown (9)	83
Tracy Tandoh (11)	83
Jodie Harding (9)	84

Laleham CE Primary School

Mia Matthews (8)	84
Maddie Payne (7)	85
Connie Boughey (7)	85
Matthew Birt (8)	86
Megan Bredo (7)	86
Alisha Brittany Rulton (8)	86
Elloise Matthews (7)	87

Christian Collins (8)	87
Lewis Ridley (8)	88
Matthew Cooper (7)	88
Emily Jaye (8)	89
Natasha Znetyniak (8)	89

St John Fisher RC Primary School, Perivale, Greenford

Reece Narang (9)	89
Louise Charles (9)	90
Nathan Byrne (9)	91
Stefan Browne (10)	92
Anna Maria Dziedzic (9)	93
Conor Coules (9)	94
Joy Tshiala (9)	94
Ramsey Badir (10)	95
Rebecca Amy Kelleher (10)	95
Richard Williams (9)	96
Maryam Ali (9)	96
Anrika Thinju (9)	97
Laurel Dunne (9)	98
Darnell Noel (10)	99
Suzy Hermiz (10)	99
Alison Gayle (10)	100
Daniel Kucharski (9)	100
Reem Gubbawy (10)	101
Patrick David (10)	101
Christopher Makar (10)	102
Jade O'Rourke (9)	102
Sterling Record (10)	103
Liam Nee (10)	103
Rebecca Okine (10)	104
Liam Mannion (10)	104
Kathrine Tyler (9)	105
Christina Symeon (8)	105
Rianna Wright Macleod (9)	106
Charlie Wright (10)	106
Domini Lovesey (10)	107
Sara-Louise Tawfig (9)	107
Jessica Tiongson (10)	108
Sarah Ishak (9)	108
Maisy Ginnelly (9)	109

Shane Carville (10)   109
Cedric Eid (9)   110
Georgia Corr (8)   110
Dana Sousa-Limbu (8)   111
Allaan Heewa (8)   111
Vikki Newbert (8)   112
Antony El-Nawar (9)   112
Aaron Walker (8)   112
Edward Deeney (9)   113
Joanna Rudzka (9)   113
Alice Starrs (9)   113
Jordan White (9)   114
Bessan Awezie (9)   114
Rahelan Ujayakamar (8)   114
Kajani Subhaskaran (7)   115
Joshua Mendonca (8)   115
Conor Tynan (7)   115
Sinead Douglas (8)   116
Aoife McGovern (7)   116
Mithun Arun Kumaran (7)   117
Ciera Walsh (8)   117
Jonathan Perera Gunathilaka (7)   117
Namir Métë (7)   118
Sean Filgate (8)   118
Kamila Fiedorczyk (8)   119
Preny Hovanessian (7)   119
Nicole Louro Serrano (7)   119
Amy Ryan (7)   120
Connor Burden (8)   120
Karalo Dunne (7)   121
Joseph Sheehan (8)   121
Daniel Siban (8)   122
David Golesz (8)   122
Martyna Rybakowska (7)   122
Tonya Likosso (8)   123

St Teresa's RC First & Middle School, Harrow Weald
Chanel Viegas (10)   123
Karen Street (11)   124
Rhys Walsh (11)   124
Hollie Ann Conway (11)   125

Ryan Dempsey (11)   125
Lewis Dickens (11)   125
James Fernandes-Pettingill (10)   126
Dominic Halpin (11)   126
Stephen May (10)   127
Shiney Rebera (10)   127
Jessica Rolewicz (11)   127
Chloe Galloway (10)   128
Antoine Brier (11)   128
Joe Watson (11)   129
Tom Wickham (11)   129
Alex Bastian (10)   129
Emily Olive (11)   130
Nathan Ball (11)   130
Nicky Geraghty (11)   131
Ryan Calder (10)   131
Tara Rahilly (10)   132
Aaron Pearce (11)   132
Rebecca Moses (10)   133
Jasmine O'Neill (11)   133
Zoë Mendez (11)   134
Alex Sheridan (10)   134
Andrew Gibbs (11)   135
Kathleen McGoldrick (11)   135
Lauren Callaghan (10)   136
Gemma Evans O'Connell (10)   136
Sinead O'Keeffe (10)   137
Niall Foxe (11)   137
Jessica Williams (11)   138
Rafaella Notarianni (10)   138
Ann-Marie Hennessy (11)   139
Jamie Wickham (11)   139
Ella Ross (10)   140
Prerak Motwany (10)   140
Tara Ryan (10)   141
Nana-Betse Parker (10)   141
Rory Carolan (10)   142
Mark Langan (10)   142
Shannen Dolan (11)   143

Springwell Junior School

Jasmeet Chana (10)	143
Natasha Mudhar (11)	144
Bhavjeet Kaur Badesha (11)	144
Akash Bhalla (11)	145
Aqib Sheikh (9)	145
Reema Kaur Uppal (11)	146
Davan Rayat (10)	147
Aleena Baig (10)	147
Humzah Baig (10)	148
Afiya Romain-Bains (10)	148
Miriam Munawar (9)	149
Kiran Sehra (9)	149
Ranjeet Nanrah (10)	150
Tara Dogra (10)	150
Faisal Qureshi (10)	150
Zak Zaheed (9)	151
Nikkita Tilwani (9)	151
Shahaan Malik (10)	151
Binisha Shah (10)	152
Navina Kaur Bagri (9)	152
Sobia Rahman (10)	153
Harjot Samra (10)	153
Reetika Kamboh (9)	154
Renuka Varma (9)	154
Shreena Acharya (9)	155
Qasim Hassan (8)	155
Jaymin Raja (10)	156
Parmveer Dhami (10)	156
Yayra Frantzen (9)	157
Mansoor Aman (9)	157
Amandeep Chauhan (9)	158
Syed Aadil Ali (9)	158
Chelsea Bailey (10)	158
Jessica Esposito (11)	159
Kayleigh Igoe (10)	160
Ilisha Haizel (9)	160
Narin Saad (10)	161
Tej Samra (9)	161
Zennub Lodhi (9)	162
Jasmin Dhamrait (9)	162

Tania Kaur Nizzar (8) — 163
Inderpreet Gill (10) — 163
Shayna Gandhi (10) — 163
Sasha Raj Dorai (11) — 164
Baldeep Ghatore (11) — 164
Inderpal Toor (10) — 165
Marc Weir (10) — 165
Luckveer Singh (11) — 166
Arron Sohota (11) — 166
Diksha Vadhera (10) — 167
Ajmeer Giasey (10) — 167
Natasha Younus (10) — 168
Puja Sharma (9) — 168
Akshay Manro (10) — 169
Paayal Gandhi (9) — 169
Harleen Mangat (9) — 170
Nina-Joyce Shehata (9) — 170
Manika Tamrat (9) — 171
Jayraj Dosanjh (8) — 171
Somya Sharma (11) — 172
Haaris Ilyas (9) — 172
Edward Murphy (10) — 173
Sukhraj Randhawa (8) — 173
Tanishar Kaur Brar (9) — 174
Duha Mohamed (10) — 174
Divya Sareen (9) — 175
Aman Ubhi (10) — 175
Amaris Lakhe (9) — 176
Steffan Green (10) — 176
Rick Kular (10) — 176
Faeza Butt (11) — 177
Rishi Dhokia (9) — 177
Amrit Ghatore (8) — 178
Sonam Dhani (9) — 178
Aaron Uraon (9) — 179
Jaspreet Gill (9) — 179
Rachael De Conto (10) — 180
Javneet Malhi (11) — 180
Ranvir Sandhu (10) — 181
Gaurav Malhi (10) — 181
Onkar Bansal (11) — 182
Amrita Gandhi (9) — 182

Demi Ryan (11)   183
Simran Khangura (8)   183
Sukhdeep Mohain (8)   183
Hira Bashir (8)   184
Simran Patel (9)   184
Hetan Dilip Bhesania (9)   184
Ibrahim Haizel (8)   185
Jaga Johal (9)   185
Avneesh Kaur Segue (11)   186
Meera Kara (9)   186
Rumneet Johal (10)   187
Dhruv Upadhyaya (8)   187
Reema Patel (10)   187
Meghana Kotipalli (9)   188
Harkaran Thind (10)   188
Maira Iqbal (9)   189
Amanjot Grewal (9)   189
Yashna Abhol (9)   190
Gurjyott Sehmi (8)   190
Pooja Amirneni (9)   191
Simran Chana (8)   191
Shivraj Aulakh (9)   192
Bhupinder Dhanoa (9)   192
Jagraj Grewal (8)   193
Vishal Bouri (9)   193
Ashanti Douglas (9)   194
Aasia Qayum (9)   195
Jay Shinhmar (9)   195
Divya Laxmi Sharma (8)   196
Lauren Chahal (8)   196
Manpreet Singh (9)   197
Shiza Amir (9)   197
Aneet Gill (8)   198
Kiran Bal (8)   198
Gubinder Sarai (9)   199
Karan Patel (9)   199
Kiranvir Gill (8)   200
Abrar Qureshi (9)   200
Rasib Shafi (8)   201
Zipo Mangaliso (10)   201
Manpreet Purewal (11)   202
Kyle Powell (8)   202

Pawandeep Bhambra (8) — 203
Tanveer Bawa (10) — 203
Ritika Sharma (10) — 204
Simran Deol (10) — 204
Satnam Mudhar (10) — 205
Payal Sharma (9) — 205
Onik Ahmed (9) — 206
Gaganjot Panesar (11) — 206
Ambika Sharma (10) — 207
Ambhar Dar (10) — 207
Zak Rahman (9) — 208
Harleen Woodwal (10) — 208
Drew Harry (8) — 208
Manvir Gill (9) — 209
Charu Abrol (9) — 209

The Poems

The Writer Of This Poem

(Based on 'The Writer of this Poem' by Roger McGough)

The writer of this poem
Is as cold as Christmas Day,
As small as an ant's finger,
As annoying as a noise that won't go away.

As funny as Krusty the Clown,
As fast as a bird,
As cheeky as a hyena,
As boring as a story you've already heard.

The writer of this poem
Never, ever gets embarrassed,
He's good at football and
He wants to go to Paris.

Jack Hayes (8)
Alpha Preparatory School

Class Poem Kennings

Amazing Anjalee
Funny Faheem
Shy Shiv
Interesting Imogen
Useful Yasmin
Kind Kamal
Active Ahmad
Pretty Prabhleen
Daydreaming Dilan
Eager Eisha
Shaking Shiv
Magic Michel
Dashing Devang
Racing Reena
Best Bhavini
Karate Krishan
Adding Abijay.

Imogen Drummond (7)
Alpha Preparatory School

The Writer Of This Poem

(Based on 'The Writer of this Poem' by Roger McGough)

The writer of this poem
Is as smooth as cream,
As tough as a football,
As lucky as my dream!

As clever as a teacher,
As bright as the sun,
As lucky as a leprechaun,
As holy as a nun.

The writer of this poem
Is as bad as a gun,
As wild as a tiger,
As annoying as a mum.

Simran Sagoo Dass (9)
Alpha Preparatory School

Class Poem Kennings

Acting Anjalee
Funny Faheem
Shy Shiv
Ill Imogen
Yapping Yasmin
Kind Kamal
Active Ahmad
Princess Prabhleen
Diving Dilan
Eating Eisha
Sewing Shiv
Miming Michel
Driving Devang
Running Reena
Basketball Bhavini
Clever Krishan
Agile Abhajay.

Yasmin Fernandes (7)
Alpha Preparatory School

The Writer Of This Poem

(Based on 'The Writer of this Poem' by Roger McGough)

The writer of this poem
Is as fat as a rat,
As stupid as a fly,
As thin as a mat.

As dirty as a baby eating,
As messy as can be,
As cheeky as a monkey,
As nosy as a pussy.

The writer of this poem
Never existed before.
He's cuter than a dog
(Or so my mum says).

Jeevan Singh (8)
Alpha Preparatory School

My Class Kennings

Active Ahmad
Acting Anjalee
Kicking Kamal
Diving Dilan
Princess Prabhleen
Shy Shiv D
Skateboarding Shiv P
Bouncing Bhavini
Running Reena
Yawning Yasmin
Football Faheem
Eating Eisha
Interesting Imogen
Miming Michel
Adding Abhijay
Cricket Krishan
Dozing Devang.

Faheem Bashir (7)
Alpha Preparatory School

The Writer Of This Poem

(Based on 'The Writer of this Poem' by Roger McGough)

The writer of this poem
Is as bright as the sun,
As wild as a tiger,
As loud as a gun.

As small as a picture,
As cheeky as a monkey,
As happy as a flower,
As quick as a bee.

The writer of this poem
Never will be rude.
She's as pretty as a princess
(Or so my mum says).

Nathalie Kelly (9)
Alpha Preparatory School

Kennings

Addictive Anjalee
   Fast Faheem
Skating Shiv
   Interesting Imogen
Useful Yasmin
   Careful Kamal
Active Ahmad
   Piping Prabhleen
Diving Dilan
   Eating Eisha
Shining Shiv
   Mighty Michel
Dashing Devang
   Reading Reena
Bendy Bhavini
   Climbing Krishan
Amused Abhijay.

Abhijay Sood (7)
Alpha Preparatory School

The Writer Of This Poem

(Based on 'The Writer of this Poem' by Roger McGough)

The writer of this poem
Has hair as black as night,
As clean as a brush,
As strong as a fight.

As fast as a hare,
As cool as a pie,
As brave as a pear,
As handsome as the sky.

The writer of this poem
Never is as important as everyone else
And if he lies, he will die
Or so a man says.

Nikhil Patel   (9)
Alpha Preparatory School

Class Poem Kennings

Agile Anjalee
Fiddling Faheem
Shivering Shiv
Impossible Imogen
Yelling Yasmin
Kicking Kamal
Active Ahmad
Princess Prabhleen
Dashing Dilan
Eeking Eisha
Shy Shiv
Master Michel
Decorative Devang
Red Reena
Bollywood Bhavini
Captain Krishan
Acrobatic Abhijay.

Bhavini M Sheth   (7)
Alpha Preparatory School

The Writer Of This Poem
(Based on 'The Writer of this Poem' by Roger McGough)

The writer of this poem
Is as clever as a crown,
As clean as a bathtub,
As cheerful as a clown.

As weeny as a grape,
As cheeky as a mosquito,
As sporty as a cheetah,
As hot as Tabasco.

The writer of this poem
Never is the same as anybody else.
She has her own personality,
She's different in the way she yells.

Samantha Carmichael (9)
Alpha Preparatory School

Kennings

Active Anjalee
Fast Faheem
Shiny Shiv D
Captain Krishan
Super Shiv P
Diving Dilan
Racing Reena
Keen Kamal
Princess Prabhleen
DJ Devang
Interesting Imogen
Archer Abhijay
Acting Ahmad
King Kamal
Young Yasmin
Mighty Michel
Beautiful Bhavini.

Shiv Patel (7)
Alpha Preparatory School

The Writer Of This Poem
(Based on 'The Writer of this Poem' by Roger McGough)

The writer of this poem
Is as tiny as a baby's finger,
As dirty as mud,
As nosy as a dog.

As messy as a hippo,
As bad-tempered as a T-rex,
As cheeky as a leprechaun,
As annoying as a hyena.

The writer of this poem
Never has a favourite.
Always good at unihoc,
Never wins a cup.

Zakariya Sheikh (8)
Alpha Preparatory School

Class Poem Kennings

Active Anjalee
Funny Faheem
Shy Shiv P
Innocent Imogen
Princess Prabhleen
Delighted Dilan
Satisfied Shiv D
Racing Reena
Merry Michel
Kicking Kamal
Useful Yasmin
Bouncing Bhavini
Acting Ahmad
Dancing Devang
Kind Krishan
Amused Abhijay
Eating Eisha.

Eisha Patel (8)
Alpha Preparatory School

The Writer Of This Poem
(Based on 'The Writer of this Poem' by Roger McGough)

The writer of this poem
Is as tall as the sky,
As clean as a washing machine,
As annoying as a fly.

As cunning as a fox,
As fast as a bullet,
As strong as an ox,
As kind as an angel.

The writer of this poem
Never wastes her days.
She's as pretty as a flower,
Or so her mother says.

Rachel Still (9)
Alpha Preparatory School

Class Poem Kennings

Angel Anjalee
Flying Faheem
Super Shiv D
Incredible Imogen
Yapping Yasmin
Kicking Kamal
Active Ahmad
Princess Prabhleen
Diving Dilan
Excellent Eisha
Springing Shiv P
Doctor Devang
Racing Reena
Busy Bhavini
King Krishan
Amusing Abhijay.

Prabhleen Oberoi (7)
Alpha Preparatory School

The Writer Of This Poem

(Based on 'The Writer of this Poem' by Roger McGough)

The writer of this poem
Is as great as a king,
As short as a wart,
As strong as a pot.

As tall as a mall,
As annoying as a tree,
As cold as a mole,
As slow as a pole.

The writer of this poem
Is never bad at everything.
He's as important as everyone else
And almost never yells.

Kayetan Shrimanker (8)
Alpha Preparatory School

My Class Kennings

Racing Rohit
Running Rupert
Active Adunni
Jumping Jay
Jogging Joey
Sensible Sachin
Rushing Rishi
Zooming Zara
Gorgeous Gurpreet
Shocking Shaquille
Sharing Shenaya
Dancing Darshana
Delightful Dilan
Clever Cameron
Crafty Kayleigh
Sport Shekinah.

Dilankumar Patel (7)
Alpha Preparatory School

The Writer Of This Poem

(Based on 'The Writer of this Poem' by Roger McGough)

The writer of this poem
Is as friendly as a cat,
As tall as a building,
As thin as a mat.

As fast as a cheetah,
As shy as a mouse,
As good as the smell of flowers,
As clean as a house.

The writer of this poem
Never tells a lie.
She's always there for others
And loves the bright blue sky.

Shria Patel   (8)
Alpha Preparatory School

My Class Kennings

Amazing Adunni
Clever Cameron
Dancing Darshana
Dashing Dilan
Gorgeous Gurpreet
Jumping Jay
Jovial Joey
Kind Kayleigh
Rushing Rishi
Racing Rohit
Rapid Rupert
Sophisticated Shenaya
Speedy Shekinah
Slow Shaquille
Short-sighted Sachin
Zooming Zara.

Gurpreet Mudhar   (7)
Alpha Preparatory School

The Writer Of This Poem
(Based on 'The Writer of this Poem' by Roger McGough)

The writer of this poem
Is taller than a house,
As tough as a tiger,
As small as a mouse.

As brave as a lion,
As cool as a disco light,
As evil as a robber,
As wicked as a knight.

The writer of this poem
Is never bad.
He's not that cheeky
And he's not that bad.

Samee Deen (9)
Alpha Preparatory School

My Class Kennings

Running Rohit
Reading Rishi
Racing Rupert
Active Adunni
Jogging Joey
Shocking Shekinah
Clever Cameron
Smiling Sachin
Dancing Darshana
Sharp Shaquille
Jaguar Jay
Shy Shenaya
Gorgeous Gurpreet
Delightful Dilan
Kind Kayleigh
Zooming Zara.

Rohit Amlani (7)
Alpha Preparatory School

The Writer Of This Poem
(Based on 'The Writer of this Poem' by Roger McGough)

The writer of this poem
Is as worrying as a baby's cry,
As quick as a jet,
As annoying as a fly.

As proud as a hippogriff,
As fast as an F1 car,
As white as chalk,
As superstitious as the god Ra.

The writer of this poem
Who likes watching rays,
Is the best at football
Or so my dad says.

Saday Lakhani (9)
Alpha Preparatory School

My Class Kennings

Dangerous Dilan
Zooming Zara
Shuffling Shaquille
Relaxing Rishi
Gorgeous Gurpreet
Shy Shenaya
Delightful Darshana
Kind Kayleigh
Active Adunni
Speedy Sachin
Reserved Rohit
Carefree Cameron
Jolly Joey
Sharing Shekinah
Retiring Rupert
Jumping Jay.

Darshana Patel (7)
Alpha Preparatory School

The Writer Of This Poem

(Based on 'The Writer of this Poem' by Roger McGough)

The writer of this poem
Is as fast as lightning,
As brave as a knight,
As bad as fighting.

As strong as a tiger,
As lazy as a sloth,
As cheeky as a hyena,
As sensitive as a moth.

The writer of this poem
Never misses his chance.
He's a great footballer and
Never wants to dance.

Rishi Gillman-Smith (9)
Alpha Preparatory School

My Class Kennings

Running Rohit
Reading Rupert
Amazing Adunni
Joyful Jay
Jogging Joey
Sensible Sachin
Rushing Rishi
Zapping Zara
Grateful Gurpreet
Super Shaquille
Successful Shenaya
Divine Darshana
Dodgy Dilan
Clever Cameron
Kissing Kayleigh
Stunning Shekinah.

Cameron Sammakieh (7)
Alpha Preparatory School

The Writer Of This Poem

(Based on 'The Writer of this Poem' by Roger McGough)

The writer of this poem
Is as cheeky as a squirrel,
As clean as a washing machine,
As clever as an owl.

As tall as a giraffe,
As chubby as cheeks,
As cheerful as a monkey,
As annoying as clattering beaks.

The writer of this poem
Is different on the outside.
She's got amazing powers
(Or has she lied?)

Anjli Patel (9)
Alpha Preparatory School

My Class Kennings

Dancing Darshana
Smart Sachin
Calm Cameron
Rich Rishi
Zooming Zara
Sharing Shekinah
Jolly Jay
Shining Shaquille
Active Adunni
Rough Rohit
Shocking Shenaya
Jogging Joey
Kind Kayleigh
Delicate Dilan
Relaxed Rupert.

Shaquille McCoy-Neil (7)
Alpha Preparatory School

The Writer Of This Poem

(Based on 'The Writer of this Poem' by Roger McGough)

The writer of this poem
Is as light as a piece of cake,
As funny as a clown
And as cheeky as a pelican.

As friendly as a good fairy,
As skinny as a skeleton,
As clean as a plain white shirt,
As slow as the traffic outside the school.

The writer of this poem
Never likes to cry.
She's addicted to the TV
And always wonders why.

Sahana Chrishanthan (8)
Alpha Preparatory School

My Class Kennings

Delightful Darshana
Shy Shaquille
Zooming Zara
Caring Cameron
Compassionate Kayleigh
Glamorous Gurpreet
Active Adunni
Restful Rohit
Shaky Shenaya
Jolly Jay
Duty Dilan
Short-sighted Sachin
Joking Joey
Remarkable Rupert
Shining Shekinah
Reliable Rishi.

Shekinah Simpson (7)
Alpha Preparatory School

The Writer Of This Poem
(Based on 'The Writer of this Poem' by Roger McGough)

The writer of this poem
Is as slow as a supermarket queue,
As tricky as a monkey,
As tall as the sky.

As kind as a bird,
As weak as paper,
As quick as a shark,
As smart as a robot.

The writer of this poem
Is never bad.
He's the best of the best
Or is he just mad?

Lanre Ige (8)
Alpha Preparatory School

Creative Classroom

Active Anjalee
Fantastic Fakeem
Shy Shiv
Independent Imogen
Yawning Yasmin
Kind Kamal
Amazing Ahmad
Princess Prabhleen
Detective Dilan
Excellent Eisha
Shiny Shiv
Marvellous Michel
Delightful Devang
Roaring Reena
Beautiful Bhavini
King Krishan
Artistic Abhijay.

Devang Shah (8)
Alpha Preparatory School

The Writer Of This Poem

(Based on 'The Writer of this Poem' by Roger McGough)

The writer of this poem
Is as tall as a skyscraper,
As cheeky as a monkey,
As thin as a piece of paper.

As brave as a lion,
As fast as sound,
As strong as a wrestler,
As hungry as a hound.

The writer of this poem
Is never the same.
He eats cheese pizzas
And is good at every game.

Ravi Achan (8)
Alpha Preparatory School

My Class Kennings

Running Rishi
Clever Cameron
Reading Rupert
Kind Kayleigh
Jumping Jay
Jogging Joey
Dancing Darshana
Shy Shekinah
Super Shaquille
Gorgeous Gurpreet
Zooming Zara
Dissatisfied Dilan
Rushing Rohit
Active Adunni
Short-sighted Sachin
Sophisticated Shenaya.

Rishi Gandhi (7)
Alpha Preparatory School

My Class Kennings

In my class there are 16 people,
They are all my friends starting with . . .

Kind Kayleigh
Dramatic Darshana
Gorgeous Gurpreet
Accelerating Adunni
Zapping Zara
Shy Shekinah
Clever Cameron
Jocular Jay
Joyful Joey
Rehearsing Rohit
Daring Dilan
Racing Rupert
Sophisticated Shenaya
Relaxing Rishi
Surprising Shaquille
Squabbly Sachin.

Shenaya Nadesan (8)
Alpha Preparatory School

Winter Acrostic Poem

W et, roaring rain.
I cy toes and fingers.
N o one can see with all the mist.
T oo cold for anyone to go outside.
E erie, exhausting, extraordinary, exhilarating winds.
R eally, really . . . really! annoying coughs and colds.

Sachin Gandhi (8)
Alpha Preparatory School

My Class Kennings

In my class there are 16 people and their names are . . .

Reliable Rohit
Racing Rupert
Adventurous Adunni
Jovial Jay
Jumpy Joey
Sophisticated Sachin
Rampaging Rishi
Zapping Zara
Generous Gurpreet
Shocking Shaquille
Sharing Shenaya
Determined Darshana
Daring Dilan K
Clever Cameron
Kind Kayleigh
Shy Shekinah
And there you have my class!

Kayleigh Simion (8)
Alpha Preparatory School

Tunisia

In Tunisia I was happy as a clam,
But when I had a sandwich I thought, *oh man!*
There was a rumble in my stomach, an aching in my guts,
So I ran to my bedroom . . . oh nuts!
So I laid in my bed for like a thousand years.
The next sunny day I was lying on the sand
Watching my happy family swimming around.
They got stung by jellyfish
So I guess I'm just lucky.

Elyar Afshari (9)
Coston Primary School

When I Went To Lebanon

When I went to Lebanon
It was so fun,
I went to the funfair
And ate a bun.

I went to posh restaurants,
It was so cool,
I went to the park
And I went to the pool.

When I went to Lebanon,
It was so nice,
I went to the mountains
And my auntie's twice.

I did loads of stuff in Lebanon,
I wish I can go again,
Not until 2006,
That's when I'm 11.

Karen Abousaleh (10)
Coston Primary School

My Jumps

When I jump in the air,
I feel like a bird flying into the sky.
When I am floating down to the ground,
I feel as light as a feather falling down.
When I jump in the sky,
I feel like a rocket shooting into the air.
When I come floating down to the ground,
I feel as heavy as a tree.

Aursh Patel (7)
Coston Primary School

My Little Brother

My little brother is a little bother,
When he pulls my hair I pretend to be a bear.
I scare him out the room,
Then I get the broom.
He tries to scare me back,
But then I get the cat.
But I can't hit him because he's too cute,
That's the problem with my little brother.

Kajal Tutt (7)
Coston Primary School

My Pet

My pet is a white rabbit,
He has pink eyes, so soft and beautiful,
Cute, white fur coat.
You touch him and he is soft.
As he hops in the garden he eats,
So he is a huge rabbit.

Lorrianne Joseph (8)
Coston Primary School

My Auntie

A untie is kind and lovely,
U nderstanding and generous,
N eat and tidy she is,
T houghtful she is,
I mpressive is her cleaning,
E very day she works hard.

Tavneet Flora (8)
Coston Primary School

My Jumps

When I jump I feel like a kangaroo jumping in the sky.
When I come down I feel like a bird's feather falling from the sky.
As I come back down I feel the wind flying back up again.

Rakim Sajero (7)
Coston Primary School

My Best Friend

My best friend is funny.
My best friend is lazy.
She is the best.
Her brother is cute.
Her brother is funny too, he laughs.
He is bored in cars.
She loves having fun.

Saif Elcafagi (8)
Coston Primary School

Roxs

Roxs, Roxs, my foxy Roxy,
She is a real, real Roxy.
If she dies at a certain age
I will make an everlasting river
And I won't stop until she comes back alive.
Roxs, oh Roxs, I love you so much.

Charlotte Nixon (8)
Coston Primary School

Kindness

Kindness lets people live in her mansion,
She shares a limousine.
Her job is to help children,
Who are orphans, that have no home.
She gives out food and clothes,
Helps old people across the road.
Her friends are friendly, happy and show-off.

Zaynah Rasheed (9)
Coston Primary School

My Big Brother

My big brother oh such a bother,
When I'm playing with my toys he teases me.
Oh! how I love my big brother,
He is funny and entertaining.
Oh! how I love my big brother.

Lulu Landers (8)
Coston Primary School

Bailey

B ig and blonde
A nd he runs around
I   don't understand
L ying on the ground
E verybody frowns
Y es he is a mad dog.

Emily Maguire (10)
Coston Primary School

Swimming

We are going on the bus,
Wherever we sit we make no fuss.
It's going to be fun,
But there's no sun.

It will be cool
When you get in the pool.
When I get out I drip,
I am very careful not to slip.

Magdalena Zamojska (8)
Coston Primary School

Acrostic Poem

W olves are special, though they eat fowl,
O n top of the mountain, the wolves howl.
L ove and cherish run in their pack,
V icious humans catch wolves in a sack.
E ver and ever wolves will live on,
S omehow though, wolves are going one by one.

Nathan Lo (10)
Coston Primary School

Bears

B ears are big and hairy,
E ven their feet are so scary.
A ll my friends say bears are big,
R unning away, chucking twigs.
S o that is a bear full of anger.

Amar Tateri (10)
Coston Primary School

The Sun

The sun is yellow,
It brightens up our day
With all its power.

The sun is a star,
Always out in the summer,
Out in the blue sky.

Giving us warmth,
Giving the flowers strength,
Making us happy.

Jessica Baradaran (10)
Coston Primary School

My Friend Adam

Adam is my best friend
And he drives me round the bend.
He likes meatballs
And he is really tall
And he always has something to mend.

Vivek Bhatti (11)
Coston Primary School

Little Girl And Her Pet

There was a little girl with her pet
And thought it was as if they'd just met.
They played a little song,
It was merry and long
And then they got caught in a net.

Nadia Mills (11)
Coston Primary School

Clumsy

Clumsy is a really funny clown,
He lives in a messy flat.
He wears a diver's suit
And he has a dustbin hat.
He doesn't have a job because
Everything he touches breaks immediately.
His boots are very long,
So he walks in a funny way.
He bumps into lamp posts.
His girlfriend Stupid is a really silly clown.

Ameer Hussain (8)
Coston Primary School

Stupid

Stupid lives in a clown tent,
He wears a driver's suit and a dustbin over his head.
His friend is Idiot,
His hobby is eating shoes.
He drinks oil and eats pencils,
He looks like a clown with a red nose.

Henry Matthews (8)
Coston Primary School

School

I like school because it's really cool.
If you don't like school, you are a fool.
I enjoy art because it's really smart.

Gaurav Prinja (8)
Coston Primary School

Winter

There is a breeze,
The winter is very cold,
Leaves fall from trees.

The trees blow,
The flowers have gone away,
Sometimes it snows.

The trees are bare,
Put gloves and scarves on
When it is winter.

Sophia Anderson Ekwere (10)
Coston Primary School

Adam

There was a young boy called Adam,
He was a real madam.
He talks in class
And never gets a pass
And walks around at random.

Narinder Thethi (10)
Coston Primary School

Friends

Friends are many,
Friends are some,
Friends are people who go and come.
Friends are people who appreciate you,
I have two; Aarti and Susmitha.

Hummera Khan (10)
Coston Primary School

My Brother

My brother is silly,
He likes a girl called Lily.
He is as thin as a pin,
He looks like a fake chin.
His hobby is to eat chilli.

Harjot Kaur Grewal (11)
Coston Primary School

Summary... Summer

The trees are still
As the birds are singing
When it is summer.

We lay in the sun
And we go on holiday
When it is summer.

We relax all day,
The summer breeze cools us
When it is summer.

Rochae Cook-Anderson (11)
Coston Primary School

Dinosaur

People don't stand a chance.
People were enjoying their dance
When they hunted them.
They destroyed Big Ben.
They killed the Prime Minister Grance.

Luke Lasenby (10)
Coston Primary School

Sunset

I look out of my window
To see the sunny colours
But nothing comes out yet.
The golden bronze, yellowy sun
Has not come out yet.
I wait for minutes, I wait for hours,
I wait for nearly a day,
But nothing comes out.
Wait! Wait! I see it! I see it!
Looking at me, I wave, it waves.
I smile at it,
It smiles at me.
Hi, my name is Sunset!
Sunset, I love to see its gleam.

Nida Shah (10)
Coston Primary School

Aliens

Aliens are green creatures
With very strange features.
Aliens are small
But some are tall.
Far, far away in the stars
Is where aliens live on Mars.
Aliens have special guns
That zap and stun.
Do you hear that humming?
The spaceship's coming.
Can you feel that air?
It's landing over there.
See that alien crew,
They're coming through.

Imran Malik (9)
Coston Primary School

School

I like to go to school
And the swimming pool
Because it's cool.
I like my classroom,
It's not gloom.
I make a friend
Until the end.
I love my lunch,
It gives me a punch.

June Digby (9)
Coston Primary School

Clever

Clever lives in a palace.
His best friend is Honest.
His favourite food is sushi with soya sauce.
Clever's favourite hobby is reading books,
His job is a professor,
He drives a spaceship,
He never gets anything wrong,
He always gets everything right.

Mohamed Ahmed (8)
Coston Primary School

Swimming

Every Tuesday we go on a bus,
Wherever we sit, we make no fuss.
I like the big pool because it's really cool.
We take a nice clean float,
Then we glide like a boat.
But be careful you don't *slip!*

Huma Shaikh (8)
Coston Primary School

My Pet Budgerigar

I have got a pet budgerigar,
He's so sweet, he'll be a star!
His name is Charlie, you should see him
Drink from his drinker, right from the brim!

When my budgie's flying he chirps really loud,
Then he flies to eat seed from the sandy ground!
After eating his meal Charlie plays with his toys,
When he rings a bell he makes so much noise!

Jennifer Rose (9)
Coston Primary School

Smelly

Smelly lives in a dump.
He always wears the same clothes,
Green trousers and green T-shirt.
He has long, black, smelly hair.
His friends are Greedy and Unhappy.
His favourite foods are garlic and raw onions.
His best car is a Ford Fiesta
And the colour of it is brown.

Bavita Tateri (8)
Coston Primary School

The Great Danes

There was a young man called Jack
Who had a brother called Mack.
They went on a plane,
They had three Great Danes
And one jumped on their back.

Jordan Luckett (10)
Coston Primary School

Swimming

We go on Tuesday, we go on the bus,
Wherever we sit we make no fuss.
When we get there we get in the pool,
But do you know it's nice and cool.

It's going to be fun,
But there's no sun.
Be careful you don't slip,
Because the teacher might flip.

Charlie Kelleher-Gibbons (8)
Coston Primary School

I Like . . .

I like swimming,
I like sports,
I like to play with dogs,
I like tigers,
I like cats,
I like to go to school,
I like playing football,
I like drawing,
I like the PlayStation.

Tillan Kailarajan (8)
Coston Primary School

Who Am I?

Cute looker,
Squeaky miaower,
Wool ripper,
Dog hater,
Good hunter,
Attention lover,
Who am I?

Melissa Neocleous (10)
Coston Primary School

Leaving

Leaving a country is a hard thing to do,
Although you don't want to, sometimes you have to.
You stand over there waving goodbye,
You might be crying but no one will care
'Cause you have to go away.
You leave your best friends behind,
As well as your house
And your school and everyone else.
You worry about what's going to happen next
And how you are going to fit in over there.

Dania Al-Khangi (11)
Coston Primary School

The Girl Who Wants To Take Over The Nation

There is a girl who wants to take over the nation
With her pet Dalmatian.
She got to the station,
She went to the next generation
On a very special occasion.

Luke Bishop (10)
Coston Primary School

Sky

I shall tell a fairy tale about the sky,
Of the sun and the moon.

The moon is closed,
The sky darkened,
Stars dripped like a soap.

Marina Shurakova (10)
Coston Primary School

My Friend Called Ben

There was a young man called Ben,
All day long he just slept with a hen.
He ran around and played all day
With his best friend called Jay
And he had another friend called Den.

Laurence Azadbakht (10)
Coston Primary School

Hannah

There was an old lady called Hannah
Who had a great big spanner.
She always walks with her clumpy feet,
She always walks down the street
And had a strange manner.

Jay-Jay Parke-Jude (11)
Coston Primary School

The Trip

We went on a trip, it was a good occasion,
We failed to reach our destination,
We walked and walked,
Some people talked
And we ended up finding a station.

Jay Strutton (10)
Coston Primary School

Night-Time

All is dark,
All is asleep,
All fast asleep.
While the wind howls
The trees rustle.
The rain tapping against the double-glazed windows
And then all of a sudden
A burst of light comes shining out.
As morning approaches the moon disappears,
Light rules over darkness.
The night fades away into sheer light
And all of a sudden the night has disappeared.

Ben House (11)
Coston Primary School

My Cat Zinger

My cat Zinger is old and fast
I get to sleep at last
She scratches my face at night
Then we start to fight
When she's alone in the house
She catches a really fat mouse
When we get back she's in front of the door
And I can see her lips are sore
I feed her and then she starts to eat
When she's finished she bites my feet
We have to stroke her lovely soft fur
And then she starts to purr.

Nadia El-Kandil (9)
Coston Primary School

I Desire Food

I love all different foods,
No matter what mood,
If I don't get any, I might get in a mood.
Chocolate, chips, cookies and ice cream with sprinkles.
Every sort of ice cream always makes me tinkle.
When I'm older I'll still eat food,
Till my skin is wrinkled, but I'll still eat Pringles.

Mark Augustine (11)
Coston Primary School

Bad Hair Day

There was a young man whose hair
Resembled a paralysed bear.
He cried all day
But would not say
That his hair was actually quite rare.

Ivana Joseph (11)
Coston Primary School

My Great Friendship (Not!)

I can't really stick my friend,
She's driving me round the bend.
I thought we'd be great,
I guess it was just fate.
Aaah! how our friendship would just end.

Sabah El-Safi (11)
Coston Primary School

Animals

Dogs like playing with logs.
Pigs like to dig.
Cats like playing with bats.
Cows like to bow.
Fish like to wash dishes.
Mice like playing with dice.

Kalelah Benjamin (7)
Coston Primary School

Family

We all need a family to keep us safe
And families can help us learn,
But the most important thing is that we all have got a family.
We also need drinks and food from our families.

L'Amour Sajero (8)
Coston Primary School

Elephant

The elephant is big and does a big stomp.
It always tears down trees when it walks.
When it eats, it eats with its cheeks puffed out.
The elephant has a big mouth and it bathes like a person.

Jounee Rodney (7)
Coston Primary School

Tiger, Tiger

Tiger, tiger in the night, in the forest burning bright.
Tiger, tiger you are stripy.
Tiger, tiger you have very bright orange stripes.

Paul Chinkwende (8)
Coston Primary School

My Sister

My sister is a rose, she likes to smell toes.
My sister is rosy, she is so, so cosy.
My sister says baddie and says Daddy.
My sister likes candy and likes to say Andy.
My sister says diddley-doo, she likes to watch Winnie the Pooh.
My sister crawls in my room, she likes to play my PlayStation 2.
My sister likes to say dummy, she loves to say Mummy!

Mickel Kruythoff (8)
Coston Primary School

Cats

Cats are small,
Cats are soft,
Cats are cute,
And cats are playful,
Cats have claws when they get angry.
Cats are fun,
And cats are smart,
And some cats are scared.
I like cats and so will you.

Christopher Redmond (7)
Coston Primary School

Snakes

Pythons are green,
Pythons are the meanest.
They can eat rats and other reptiles,
They are very cunning like the red fox.
They are the biggest
And they can poison us.

Khaleel Begg (7)
Coston Primary School

Apples Are Red, Apples Are Green And Apples Are Yellow

Apples are red
Apples are green
Apples are yellow
Apples are juicy and sometimes they are dirty
And sometimes they are very dry
Sometimes they have brown on them, when they're old.

Harseen Khailany (7)
Coston Primary School

Basketball

Basketball; circular and grippy,
as round as a globe.
Looks like an orange, shaped like the world.
It's a good sport and a fun activity,
you'll have so much fun
and such a good time.
I'll get past anyone, tall or small,
I'll dazzle them and shoot with the ball.

Tevin Williamson (10)
Coston Primary School

Blondi The Incredible Hamster

Sleepy Blondi in my hat
Squeaking like a little rat
Makes me smile
Giggle too
Makes me sleepy
Just like her.

Mariam Polad (9)
Coston Primary School

Famous

When I'm famous I'll be rich,
I'll be able to do anything, like turn into a witch.
When I'm famous I'll live in a mansion,
It'll be big with a loft extension.
When I'm famous I'll be the best,
Better and smarter than all the rest.
But at the moment that is just a dream,
A special, twinkling, shining dream.

Sammy Kaur Sidhu (9)
Coston Primary School

Loving It

Playing chase in the pool with my brother,
Screaming in my ear, warm water on my toes.
Shock going down the big slide with water,
After swimming I went to McDonald's
And had a burger, it was delicious,
I then went home.

Amy Nixon (10)
Coston Primary School

Zain

There was a young boy called Zain
He really was a pain
Outside in the park
Falling over in the dark
Walking home down the lane.

Mustafa Mohammed (10)
Coston Primary School

Snakes

Scared, frightened I was in a terrible state,
but afterwards I felt very brave
and now I want to do it again.
Scaly, flexible, long and legless too.
They are shy and long, waiting for you to be gone.
You think you're scared of them,
but they are misunderstood,
they're more scared of you.
You think they're slimy, if you think that, blimey!
They're smooth and scaly with a tongue that flickers,
each flicker a silent death appears.

Owen Kelley Patterson (9)
Coston Primary School

My Bedroom

Nice, cosy and a loving place.
Cool and fun, I play all day.
My nice quilt makes me feel safe and warm.
Sky blue walls make me feel outside.
Precious things I love.
Friendship to my best friends.

Anthony Francis (10)
Coston Primary School

Poem Sentences

I can run and ride and skate and play,
And it is good and I am fit.
Snowflakes are big,
And sometimes they are small and good.

Farhan Khan (7)
Coston Primary School

Hurricane Francis

Hurricane Francis was really, really low.
All my family had to sleep in the bathroom
and it smelt really bad.
The floor was cold and it was really hot
with eight people in a small bathroom.
My cousin was so scared, she started to cry.
I was in a bungalow.
I heard the wind circling the bungalow.
It was really shocking.

Joel Hamilton (10)
Coston Primary School

When I Went To Chessington

It was fun, dragon's fury is like having fun.
Scared is like a child screaming.
Joyful is having fun.
Run is like the speed of a child.
Eating pizza like a rumbling tummy.
Wet is like swimming in the water.
Scary rides is like the crying of a child.
Fun rides, cool rides, we love it.

Zeshan Khalid (10)
Coston Primary School

My Jumping Poem

I can jump as high as a tree.
I can jump as high as a pig and a kangaroo.
I can jump, you can jump, everyone can jump.
I can jump, jump, jump like a frog.

Olivia McLeod (7)
Coston Primary School

When I Jump

When I jump I am a grasshopper
And when I go down I am myself
When I jump I am a bird and I go down
I am a feather from the earth
When I jump I am a parrot as feathery as a bush
And when I go down I am a tree
When I jump I am a kangaroo
And when I go down I am a bed.

Sam House (6)
Coston Primary School

My Jump

When I jump I feel like I am as light as a feather
The wind blows on me, the breeze is gentle
It's soft, very soft, I feel relaxed
When I jump, lovely in the breeze
It's quite relaxing, it's kind of fun
Jumping down from the sky
I feel soft too.

Taran Sidhu (6)
Coston Primary School

Jumps

When I jump up into the sky
I feel like a rabbit in the sky
When I come back down I feel like a leaf fluttering down
When I jump up as high as the sky
I can feel the sky pushing me down
When I jump I feel like a frog in the pond.

Ricky Heavans (7)
Coston Primary School

Rabbits

Rabbits, rabbits in the sky,
Rabbits, rabbits jumping by.
Rabbits, rabbits shouting from high,
Rabbits, rabbits rubbing their thigh.
Rabbits, rabbits being very sly,
Rabbits, rabbits eating their pie.
Rabbits, rabbits sleeping in their bed,
Rabbits, rabbits, there it's said.

Devna Patel (7)
Coston Primary School

Jumps

I can jump really high.
I can jump really low.
When I jump up I feel like I'm an angel flying.
When I jump down I feel like a piece of paper falling down.
I can jump,
You can jump,
Everyone can jump.

Kiah Sylvan (7)
Coston Primary School

Family Jumps

My dad can jump higher than a rabbit.
When I jump, I jump higher and higher until I'm in the sky.
My mum can jump up to Heaven and space.
My mum can jump so high that she can be higher than me.
My dad can jump like a kangaroo.

Diane-Louie Baker-Dee (6)
Coston Primary School

When I Jump

When I jump I am bigger than my mum.
When I am falling down it feels like I am falling down a mountain.
When I jump I can see the world.
But when I am falling I feel like I am a leaf falling from a tree.

Sulaymaan Dar (6)
Coston Primary School

My Family

F riendly, fun, kind are my family.
A lways funny and tells me jokes.
M ost important to me.
 I f I was ill my mum would help me.
L ovely and beautiful my family.
Y ells some of the time.

Rachel Duke (7)
Coston Primary School

When I Jump . . .

When I jump I feel like I'm flying.
When I jump I'm like a tall tree.
When I jump I give a big bang
And I clap my hands with joy.

Xena Hawkins (6)
Coston Primary School

My Dad

My dad
He lets me have anything I want
When I am doing my homework
He bakes a pie.

Parth Patel (7)
Coston Primary School

My Sister

S ometimes she is kind.
I like her so much.
S ee her drawing, it's the best.
T ells me words when I am reading,
E ver so pretty.
R eally beautiful and sweet.

Sadia Shafi (7)
Coston Primary School

Boastful Ben

Ben boasts all the time, no wonder
He doesn't know how to rhyme
He boasts in the morning
He boasts in the night
He boasts to give people a fright.

Sarah Glenton (7)
Coston Primary School

My Brother

My brother plays nice games with me
I love my brother, he makes me laugh
My brother loves me and I love him too
And he plays football.

Renee Francis (7)
Coston Primary School

Frogs Jump

Frogs jump in the sky
From the ground
To the sky.

Joshua Gaunt (6)
Coston Primary School

My Sweet Leticia

My little sister plays with combs.
My little sister loves to be a tomboy.
My little sister Leticia plays with a knife and fork.
My little sister Leticia likes so much.
My little sister Leticia touches my big sister's hair.
My little sister Leticia doesn't like Mum doing her own hair.

Dannieller Lemiare (7)
Coston Primary School

The Idiom Poem!

My aunt says,
'You're wrapped around my finger.'
(But I don't fit.)

My mum says,
'Keep your eyes peeled.'
(Mine wouldn't come off.)

My dad says,
'Take a biscuit.'
(But he never offers me one.)

Some people say,
'I'm over the moon.'
(I can't jump that high.)

Everyone says,
'Keep your hair on.'
(But it never drops.)

When my sister laughs
She drives me round the bend.
(I bumped into another car.)

Sinthusan Gunaratnam (10)
Dormers Wells Junior School

What Do We Do?

Dad said,
He was feeling under the weather,
(I put the weather channel on.)

Mum said,
She was as right as rain,
(I gave her an umbrella.)

Dad said,
He was sleeping like a log,
(I was going to put him on fire.)

My friend said,
'You're worth her salt,'
(I gave her a full bag of salt.)

People say,
Down in the dumps,
(I found my teacher there.)

Renu Shoor (9)
Dormers Wells Junior School

The Playground

The playground is a place of fun,
The playground is a place to talk.
The playground is a place to run,
The playground is a place to walk.

But today when I went to the playground,
I noticed something different.

The playground was now a place of cruelty,
Children pushing, children bullying.
The playground is now a place of dishonesty,
Children crying, children hurting.

So if the playground is a place of cruelty,
How can it be a place of fun?

Muhammad Hasan (10)
Dormers Wells Junior School

Idiom Poem

My mum said
to keep my eyes peeled.
I tried, but it stung.

My dad said
not to wind my sister up.
How can I, I haven't got a key?

Gran's friend said
to me to stop turning on my charm.
How can I, I haven't got a switch?

My auntie said to me
not to stir up my brother.
How can I, I haven't got a spoon?

My brother came in and said
it was raining cats and dogs.
I went to get one, I didn't see any.

Priya Sharma (9)
Dormers Wells Junior School

My Poem

I looked outside
It was raining cats and dogs
I went outside and got one for my mum.

I was told
To keep my eyes peeled
It really hurts.

People keep their
Fears inside them
I kept mine in a jar.

My mum said,
'Let's grow a family tree.'
I said, 'Can I stick myself on?'

Akshay Patel (10)
Dormers Wells Junior School

The Idiom Poem

The teacher said,
'It's raining cats and dogs.'
(I had to close the window.)

My aunty stayed over,
She sleeps like a log.
(I was about to light a fire.)

My family and I went out,
We painted the town red.
(The neighbours were surprised.)

My friend said,
'I'm down in the dumps.'
(No wonder she stank.)

My dad said,
'I'm over the moon!'
(I guess he needed stilts.)

Puneet Bhachu (10)
Dormers Wells Junior School

Sounds Good!

The smallest sound in the world is
A mouse squeaking.

The spookiest sound in the world is
Hearing footsteps behind me.

The noisiest sounds in the world are
Bangs and screeches of fireworks.

The happiest sound in the world is
My friends laughing.

Vickram Singh (9)
Dormers Wells Junior School

Idiom Poem

My mum said,
'It's raining cats and dogs.'
(I stepped in a poodle.)

My brother said
He was down in the dumps.
(I found my friend there.)

My uncle said
He was over the moon.
(Did you see an astronaut there?)

My dad said,
'Let's grow a family tree.'
(Can I grow myself on there?)

My teacher said,
'And your cousins are like peas in a pod.'
(I like the idea of being green.)

My auntie is
A terrible name dropper.
(It takes forever to sweep them up.)

Amardeep Dosanjh (9)
Dormers Wells Junior School

Sounds

The smallest sound in the world is
A snail slithering by.

The spookiest sound in the world is
Someone screaming in the middle of the night.

The noisiest sound in the world is
When a baby is crying.

The happiest sound in the world is
A bird singing in the trees.

Hasib Mahmoud (8)
Dormers Wells Junior School

The Idiom Poem

Dad said,
'You're a chip off the old block.'
(They tasted nice.)

Mum said,
'It's raining cats and dogs.'
(I suggested we let them in.)

Some people say
They're down in the dumps.
(I found my teacher there.)

Auntie said,
'Keep your eyes peeled.'
(It did hurt.)

When my uncle laughs
He drives me up the hill
(I always slide back down.)

Jaathushan Ganesapathy (10)
Dormers Wells Junior School

Sounds

The tiniest sound in the world is
A buttercup flapping its wings.

The spookiest sound in the world is
A ghost whispering in my room.

The noisiest sound in the world is
A drum banging over and over.

The happiest sound in the world is
A cat purring.

Ikram Musse (8)
Dormers Wells Junior School

My Idiom

My dad told me
Not to drop names
(I was wondering how to sweep them up.)

My mum told me
It would be raining cats and dogs
(I couldn't really see any.)

My uncle told me
Not to let the cat out of the bag
(Too late, it was gone.)

The detective told me
To keep my eyes peeled
(Now that *hurt.)*

My brother told me
To hold my tongue
(It was too slippery.)

Qasim Farid (10)
Dormers Wells Junior School

Love

Soft red rose,
Warm breeze floating by.
Tingly feeling from head to toes,
Wind whispering in the sky.

The sun is smiling,
The clouds are dancing.
Singing quietly,
My heart flying free.

Everything is alive,
My breath takes a dive.
White as a dove,
I'm in love.

Roop Bhinder (9)
Dormers Wells Junior School

Playtime Poem

Fun, fun every day,
I like to run,
I like to play.

I like to play football with my friends
Even though they don't want to play.

I like to have fun,
I like to talk,
I like to run,
I like to walk.

I don't like rain days,
I only like plain days,
I don't like to go to the school hall,
I like to play football next to the wall.

I hate wet play,
The teacher won't let us go outside.

I feel so sad when my belt falls
On the playground.

Abdi Adnan   (10)
Dormers Wells Junior School

Playground Fun

Playground, playground, grey as the ground,
Playground, playground, I can hear a sound.

Children, children, jump up and down,
Children, children, run round and round.

Teacher, teachers, wave your stick,
Teacher, teacher, be very strict.

Bell, bell, are you really well?
Bell, bell, you have a really good smell.

Aamina Deen   (9)
Dormers Wells Junior School

Bottling Up!

My friends are
Peas in a pod.
(I try to eat them, but I fail.)

The detective said that the keys
Were out of order.
(I went to the judge to ask why?)

My brother said that
It's raining cats and dogs.
(I'll try not to step in a poodle.)

My cousin said that I had
My head in the clouds.
(The lightning gave an electric shock.)

My auntie said to
Bottle up my feelings.
(I keep mine in a bottle.)

My dad is a terrible
Name dropper.
(I help my mum sweep them up.)

My mum said that
My teacher went bananas.
(I slipped on the skin.)

My teacher said that
I can have a free hand.
(Now I've collected six.)

Shangavee Sivaselvaraja (10)
Dormers Wells Junior School

Sparkling Night

Sparkling night,
Sparkling moon,
Sparkling stars.
When morning comes
The shiny sight,
Shiny sky,
Shiny sun,
Shiny clouds.
When the moon
Rises the sun will go.
Sparkling night,
Sparkling moon,
Sparkling stars.
The sun will rise
And the moon will go
Shiny sun,
Shiny sky,
Shiny clouds.
Sparkling
Day
And
Night!

Bijal Patel (9)
Dormers Wells Junior School

Diwali

Diwali is the festival of light,
Such a beautiful sight.
The fireworks go bang!
Such beautiful colours.
The divas on the wall.
Sparks from fireworks fall.
I see them through my bedroom window.

Simrandeep Gill (9)
Dormers Wells Junior School

The Visible Beast!

A frozen-footed monster
Is coming this way.

Why couldn't it come another day
Or maybe another way?

But now the monster's here,
Eating fruit and drinking beer.

It might hurt the lovely park,
When it's midnight dark.

At night he took someone's silly hat,
Ate it all up and became much too fat.

He became very red,
When he started to be much too fed.

Now the visible beast
Is going back to his own feast!

Manpreet Kaur Rajbans (8)
Dormers Wells Junior School

The Playground

The bell rings,
The children rush out to the playground,
Some hold skipping ropes,
Some holding balls.
Screaming and shouting, children everywhere,
Waving their hands in the air.
Footballs flying from side to side,
Girls running to find places to hide.
Girls skipping faster and faster,
Boys screaming louder and louder.
The sound of the bell makes everyone freeze,
No one even dares to sneeze.
They all then line up and go to their classes,
Some getting ready to put on their glasses.

Sara Haider (10)
Dormers Wells Junior School

Can You Guess Who My Love Is?

My love, my love,
Is as beautiful as a dove.
She shines like the sun
And that's the way it's done.
So can you guess who my love is?

She makes me food
And I get rude.
She shows her manners
While someone hammers.
So can you guess who my love is?

She flies like a bird
And runs like a herd.
She sings like rings
And rules the kings.
So can you guess who my love is?

That's right,
It's my grandma.

She's a fantastic, funny grandma,
Great, gorgeous Grandma.
She's the best grandma in the world.

Zahra Deen (8)
Dormers Wells Junior School

Love Poem

My love for football when Man United wins,
See Ronaldo doing his skills, the excitement kicks in,
When we're winning one-nil.

Ryan Giggs doing his step over but does not fall over!
Gary Neville's the defender, he's spinning like a blender.

Alan Smith is the Man United striker but he's like a fierce tiger.
Scholes and Miller in midfield carrying the Manchester United shield.

Devesh Sharma (9)
Dormers Wells Junior School

Playground

The playground is fun,
The playground is a place to run.

We always have time to jump around
In the playground.

We twist, we turn,
We skip and jump as we learn
And we are always there.

We are all around
In the middle of the town.

The playground is colourful,
The playground is bright.

Most places are green,
Like the bushes and trees.

I see the green plant where
It has fully grown in the playground.

Huda Hassan (10)
Dormers Wells Junior School

Wintry Nights

One dark, frosty night
Children have a snowball fight,
Slippery, slimy, snowy snow,
Snowy ice as white as white,
You've never seen such a white sight.

Trees are dying, flowers are crying
Under the snow,
Under the snow.

Icy icicles under the window sill,
Animals say cheerio to the snow.

Some people inside eating their soup,
Some people upstairs on the loo,
But everyone knows the snow we know.

Maryam Naz (9)
Dormers Wells Junior School

An Acrostic Wrestling Poem

W restling is simply the best,
O rton was champ, Triple H did the rest.
R VD, high-flying daredevil,
L ittle Rey Mysterio will keep it at a level that's
D emented.

W orld Wrestling Entertainment with
R andy Orton, youngest ever world champ,
E ric Bischoff who is RAW's GM,
S uperstars, more than 100 of them.
T ing, ting, ting for the bell,
L ast Ride Match, The Undertaker Vs JB,
I C Champion: Who will it be? John Cena or even Kenzo Suzuki.
N ever try to fight Kane; Gene Snitsky knows that well,
G oldberg is the wrestler who used to play in the NFL.

E ven wrestling comes to England to keep us happy with
N idia who should wear a nappy.
T iger bombs by Rodney Mack,
E ric Bischoff will give you the sack.
R ic Falir: 'Woooooooooooo!'
T est - will give you the big boot and the test drive too.
A Train will put you in a train wreck.
I ntercontinental champion is Chris Jericho.
N icholai Volkovff, a Russian Hall of Famer!
　 But some will just say 'So.'
M r McMahon, chairman of WWE.
E dge is even better than Spike Dudley.
N ever try this at home unless you want a broken neck,
T omorrow you'll feel like you've been in a train wreck.

Harvind Khosa (9)
Dormers Wells Junior School

Love

(To my parents)

I love the wind through my hair,
To chase circling leaves,
To feel the warmth of your touch,
Like the gentle breeze.
I love your soft kisses upon my head,
Those quiet moments we spend,
The child within you when we play,
The comfort you give me when you tuck me into bed.
I love your unconditional love,
You are my comfort,
My angel sent from above.
I give to you
My gratitude,
My heart,
My love.

Saleh Zaheer (8)
Dormers Wells Junior School

Winter

Frosty, snowy, icy, dark,
Very cold in the grassy park.
Slippery, icy, dark and cold,
A child making a snowman mould.
Glittering, gleaming ice,
That looks like a sparkling spice.
Sparkly snow in white,
With nothing else in sight.
Lots of snow in the trees,
Small ice drops the size of fleas.
The snow melts away at the end of the day.

Lincy Fernandez (9)
Dormers Wells Junior School

A Poem About Love

Every time you talk to me, I don't know what to say,
Because everything you say to me, takes my breath away.
I can't express my feelings because you have stolen all my heart,
The thought of us not together tears my world apart.
When I'm with you, it's almost more than I can take,
It feels like I'm dreaming, and I never want to wake.
I never want to lose you, I always want you there,
Always there to lean on, always there to care.
'Forever and for always,' just isn't long enough.
So keep it for eternity or for just another day,
But no matter how long you want it, my love is here to stay.
So every time I have to leave and give you one more kiss,
Think about the words I've said and please remember this,
. . . As time goes on together I know our love will grow . . .
. . . By the way, I never really told you, but you had my
Love from hello.

Manish Pandey (8)
Dormers Wells Junior School

Playground Poem

Skipping, jumping, running around,
Hide-and-seek makes no sound.

Dinner ladies, girls and boys,
Children playing with their toys.

Tamagotchis and scoubidous,
They are banned, it's the latest news.

Basketballs rocketing through the air,
Bullying is just not fair.

The bell rings for us to go in
And put our rubbish in the bin.

Daniela Bertoglio, Danielle Fenwick, Madeleine Dave,
Emma Burrows & Melissa Soden (10)
Echelford Primary School

My Magic Box
(Based on 'Magic Box' by Kit Wright)

I will put in my box,
The silk of a silver, shimmering star,
A carpet of dreams dripping in dream drops,
The petal of a flower covered in morning dew.

I will put in my box,
The tooth of a tiger that once tore up meat,
A cute cat climbing up curtains,
A dolphin diving into a bath full of water.

I will put in my box,
The soft touch of a first kiss,
The silky smoothness of babies' skin.

I will put in my box,
The thirteenth month and the tenth planet,
A fish flying through the clouds,
A cat swimming loudly through the deep blue sea.

My box is made of
Dazzling diamonds twinkling at you as you walk by,
Enchanting emeralds, blood-red rubies
And the hinges are made of gold from our own Queen's crown.
It is covered in a silk gown.

I shall fly on my box
Through the jungles of the world,
Helping animals and people,
As I fly and make a rainbow
The colour of a prism
For all to see!

Katherine Church (10)
Echelford Primary School

My Angel

My angel is in my dreams, so nice and kind,
The angel so nice and kind still in my mind,
My worries go away when I hear my angel fluttering away,
Every word I say she obeys,
I listen to her speech with a gentle kind voice,
But when the bullies come to tease I think of my angel.
The angel in my dreams is not a bad angel, it is a good angel,
Each day I give her a present that she likes,
In my dreams I would fly with her past all the planets and stars,
But nothing is going to stop me from imagining my angel,
But will anyone?

Alexandra Dennis (8)
Echelford Primary School

Weekdays, Weak Days

Monday is muddle day,
Getting muddled up day.

Tuesday is tube day,
Getting the tube day.

Wednesday is wedding day,
Getting married day.

Thursday is curd day,
Eating lemon curd day.

Friday is my day,
All eyes on me day.

Saturday is chatter day,
Chatting all day long.

Sunday is fun day,
Having a fun day.

Charley Jagger (9)
Echelford Primary School

Play Routine

The bell rings,
Time for play,
Darting and diving,
Running away.
A trip to the hall,
A bite for lunch,
Sucking up drinks,
An apple crunch.
See my friends,
Join in for a game,
George felt ill,
Won't be the same.
Starting to get tired,
Sit down for a rest,
Talk for a while,
Play's the best.
Up I am,
Ready to go,
This I'm sure of,
Believe me I know.
The end of play,
The finish of games,
Back inside,
Freedom up in flames.

Thomas Wyse Jackson (11)
Echelford Primary School

Captured Inside Me Is . . .

A long aeroplane travelling through the fluffy white clouds,
The sweet sound of tiny birds at sunset,
The fresh smell of freshly baked bread in the baker's shop,
The long palm trees swaying gently on a tropical island,
The gentle breeze falling on my face when I go skiing,
The calm waves through the shimmering sea.

Eloise Hutchins (9)
Echelford Primary School

Captured Inside Me Is . . .

A big long palm tree
Sprawling across the floor.

The nice strong breeze
Shivering across your head.

Some little robins singing
In the lonely trees.

You're crashing through the snow
While the snow is falling on your head.

The lovely smell of fresh bread
Waiting on the counter for you.

The shiny gold shadows on your head.

Alice Dowdeswell (8)
Echelford Primary School

Dog

As furry as a gorilla,
As cute as a snake,
As cuddly as a rabbit.

Ears like little teacups,
Fast like a champion,
Hungry like a lion,
Tail like a bit of string,
A wet nose like a little stream.

As small as two dinner plates,
As jumpy as a chimpanzee.

Legs like little bits of iron
And sleeps like a hedgehog.

Lucy Butler (8)
Echelford Primary School

Weekdays, Weak Days

Monday is done day,
Done all my homework day.

Tuesday is tube day,
Telling jokes to the tube day.

Wednesday wedding day,
Working as a waitress at a wedding day.

Thursday is curd day,
Eating lemon curd day.

Friday is dye day,
Dying my hair today day.

Saturday is matter day,
Saying, 'What's the matter day?'

Sunday is Monday,
Getting near to Monday day.

Sophie Lock (8)
Echelford Primary School

Pollution Acrostic

P olluted river full of polystyrene bobbing down the river,
    towards the sea,
O ut goes the wildlife and the o-zone layer.
L et's try and help to save the world.
L ovely flowers being destroyed by poison,
U ntidy litter on the streets and the hills.
T ar in seas and on the beach,
I magine the world differently.
O ver the world the pollution spreads,
N ever can we tidy up this mess.

Natalie Butler (9)
Echelford Primary School

Captured Inside Me

A tropical paradise overlooking
The horizon of Hawaii.

Six acid spitting snakes
Cornering me side to side.

The sweetness of a chocolate bar
Being opened for the very first time.

The sunflower majestically
Standing and proud.

The sweet fragrant smell
Of a bloomed rose.

A lion protecting his territory fiercely.

An old man cruelly hitting
A poor, innocent little child.

One beautiful soaring eagle
Whispering through the air.

The marvellous taste of golden fish fingers.

The thought of you in the death-crying
Forest at twelve o'clock at night.

Lucy Hickman (9)
Echelford Primary School

Animal Poem

Its feathers are as soft as a pillow,
Its beak as sharp as a needle,
It flies swiftly like a glider,
It hunts like a hungry leopard flying over the vast mountains,
It flies as fast as a jet plane,
It lives on a flag,
Its tail is as triangular as a spaceship.
Can you guess who I'm talking about?

Tom Hunt (8)
Echelford Primary School

The Listeners

He banged on the door,
He turned the rusty handle,
The door creaked open slowly,
He walked in and the door slammed behind him,
He fell on the rusty floorboards
And shouted,
'I shouldn't have let them send me to war,
Why, why, why?'
He heard a noise,
He turned around,
He started walking up the staircase,
He got halfway.
'Help.'
Bang - he fell to the floor.
He looked,
There were cobwebs,
Taps leaking,
Bats squeaking,
A chill ran down his back,
'You are too late - we all caught the plague.'
He ran,
Jumped on his horse and clattered away
Forever!

Adam See (10)
Echelford Primary School

Captured Inside Me

Captured inside me is . . .
A tall palm tree swaying majestically in the gentle breeze,
A golden eagle soaring through the air,
A tall giraffe munching on some juicy leaves,
A frozen lake reflecting the golden sunlight,
The long grass swaying in the wind.

Sean McCarthy (9)
Echelford Primary School

Weekdays, Weak Days

Monday is mud day,
Getting in the mud day.

Tuesday is twos day,
Eating two of everything day.

Wednesday is weed day,
Collecting weeds day.

Thursday is burst day,
When we pop balloons day.

Friday is fly day,
When we all try to fly day.

Saturday is snack day,
Having lots of snacks day.

Sunday is sunbed day,
Lying in the sun day.

Emma Stubbs (9)
Echelford Primary School

Captured Inside My Head

Captured inside my head is . . .
A humongous swimming pool all the way in another country,
Where the fresh smell of coconuts in the trees
And the sound of the planes passing by in the sky.
But in the jungle lay the jaguar, black panther and cheetah,
All waiting for their prey to come out.
One's in the tree,
One's in the bush
And one's on a man's roof waiting for you!

Daniel Nielsen (8)
Echelford Primary School

A Mystery Animal

As fluffy as cotton wool,
As playful as a child,
As cute as a newborn baby,
Naughty like a bully at school,
Whiskers like a fully grown pencil,
As smelly as a foot,
As shy as a turtle,
As sleepy as a koala bear,
As cuddly as a teddy bear,
Eyes like a mirror,
As quick as a cheetah.

Who am I?

Jemma Pearce (8)
Echelford Primary School

Captured Inside Me Is . . .

The clickety click, click
Of the vampire and the python
Climbing their tall, long hill.

A newborn kitten rolling
Crazily on the floor
With its pink, round ball.

Seeing an animal being
Treated unpleasantly.

Being shut in a room that is
As dark as the midnight sky
With the fear of a ghost appearing.

Georgia Phillips (9)
Echelford Primary School

The Listeners

He knocked on the door a third time,
Walked back,
Pushed the door,
It opened,
It creaked again!
'Mum, Dad, anybody,
I'm here.'
No one answered,
All he could see was cobwebs,
Over the stairs,
On the windows,
It was like curtains that were white.

He felt a tap on his shoulder,
He turned around,
No one was there,
He went into the living room,
He saw them,
They were there.
He went over to say hello,
Then they disappeared
Into nothingness,
He screamed,
Aaaaah!
He went upstairs to the bedroom
With the stairs
Creaking and creaking!

Emily Brambleby (10)
Echelford Primary School

The Listeners

He banged on the door,
He turned the handle,
It opened very slowly,
And it creaked a lot,
He turned around,
The door closed,
He stepped inside,
And fell to the floor,
I shouldn't have left them
To go to war,
Why? Why? Why?

The house had
Dripping water,
Splattering from the tap,
Fluffy cobwebs and was very dark,
I shouted, 'Is anybody in? Hello!'
'Come upstairs,' shouted a hollowing voice,
He went upstairs,
His family were dead,
A voice from behind muttered,
'You're too late!'
'No!'
'Your mother is a ghost,'
'No she's not, you're lying!'
The cobwebs were as fluffy as a cat,
'Why do you have to do this to me?'
The ghost said, 'I will kill you if you don't shut up,'
'Don't tell me to shut up,'
A knife sliced across his stomach,
He was dead,
He was laid next to his father,
For eternity!

Danny Woods (10)
Echelford Primary School

Sidney

Sidney is the meanest scorpion,
Covered in leather and chains,
Who hangs at the old station,
He is the king of bling, hiding in the trains.

At Clawford School,
He was always cool,
He hated the head of school.

Now he wears diamond things,
In charge of Scorpio blings,
His favourite food is crab,
With seafood kebab.

He hates the crabsters,
Always eating hamsters,
Lead by the Japanese spider crab.

Thomas Giles (10)
Echelford Primary School

Coco

She's as soft as a sheepskin coating.
She's light like a handbag.
She sleeps silently in the night like an ant walking.
My pet is really talented at howling
In the middle of the night.
She is super at running.
She's so rapid and so noiseless.

Rory Thomas (9)
Echelford Primary School

The Listeners

He banged on the door a third time,
Then he turned the door knob,
As the door opened, it creaked,
He slowly tip-toed in,
Suddenly the door slammed
No!
He fell to the floor,
Cried and shouted,
Why did I leave and go to war?
Why?

While he was crying he noticed all the cobwebs,
The walls were cracking,
Rats were scampering around,
And the floor was falling apart,
He heard some cackling upstairs,
The traveller ran up there,
He looked around,
Stood still,
And then his wife appeared as a ghost!
She said 'You're too late,
It's not the same
Anymore!
We can't see each other till you die.'
The traveller said, 'But . . . '
And she vanished,
No!
He was so gutted and sad,
So he ran downstairs,
Jumped on his horse and went.

Dean Horsburgh (10)
Echelford Primary School

The Listeners

He banged on the door a third time,
And then he pushed on the door,
The large, brass knocker swung from side to side,
The door flew back and crashed against the wall,
He entered the house,
Slowly,
It was draughty,
Dust hanging everywhere.

He sat on the wooden steps and cried,
'If only the war hadn't taken me away,' he sobbed,
He walked up the big stairs,
And saw a half-lit candle lying on the floorboards.

Something pulled on his shirt,
Nothing there,
He turned the other way,
Nothing there,
'It's me,' a voice murmured,
'Who's there?' The traveller saw some ghosts,
'You're too late,' the faint ghost said,
'We died of the plague. You will never meet me again
Until they get out your *coffin!*'
Daddy!
He looked down, he saw his 2 year old daughter,
'Come here,' he shouted,
Bang!
They vanished like the sun,
He went slowly back out the door,
And climbed onto his big, black stallion,
He galloped, galloped and galloped away,
Never to return to his haunted house again.

Becky Ware (10)
Echelford Primary School

The Listeners

He knocked again for a third time
And the door loudly creaked.
He pushed it open slowly
As the rain on the window streaked.

'If only I had come back sooner,'
He called in a low tone,
As the floorboards made a sound like quiet lightning,
And he heard a high-pitched moan.

It said, 'Why didn't you call?'
'I would if I had had a chance,'
He answered looking around,
On the floor there were swords and a broken lance.

'What happened here?' he asked.
They came - the whole lot,
Who was it - the war?
And now they're making a plot.

Suddenly out jumped a whole lot of men,
Charging at him with sharp swords,
They jumped on him, threw him to the ground,
And tied him up with chains and cords.

Then he joined them,
His family and friends,
He was quite glad he was with them
Because that's where his life ends.

Hayleigh Whiteside (10)
Echelford Primary School

The Listeners

He banged on the door a third time
The door flew open with a loud bang.

As he walked into the gloomy hallway
The door slammed
A huge cloud of dust
Blew into his face
He started to cough.

The floorboards creaked
He walked into the living room
A shiver went down his spine.

He heard a creak
There was no one to be seen
Suddenly *Boo!*

It was a ghost!
He felt a hand on his shoulder,
It was his wife.

She said,
'We caught a disease
You were at war,
I'm so sorry!'

She disappeared without a trace.

He jumped on his horse and rode away,
Full of sadness and regret,
The traveller would never again see her face,
And he was never seen again.

Megan Lewis (10)
Echelford Primary School

The Haunted House

He knocked a third time,
Even louder,
But still nobody answered,
He pushed open the door,
There was nobody there!

He took a few steps forward into the house,
The floorboards creaked,
Like nails on a chalkboard.

He walked through a door that was half open,
The old library,
He started reading,
Suddenly,
A big bang came from across the house.

He went there;
The living room,
Something tapped him on the shoulder,
A ghost!

He stared,
The ghost spoke,
It was his wife,
Long since dead.

'I am sorry that I went to war,
I will never see you in this life again!'

He turned
Walked wistfully away,
Jumped on his horse,
And rode away
Never to return!

Jonathan Aspin (10)
Echelford Primary School

My Dad

Dad's like a beaver building our toys,
Fixing and mending the house.

Very loud like jazz,
With an echoing voice.

A hedgehog with a thorny moustache,
Never sleeping at night.

He's calm, he's like mint ice cream,
A tiny bit hot.

Sleeps and snores,
As loud as a train going by.

Head through the clouds,
As tall as a mini bus.

I love my dad.

Safia Ballout (9)
Edward Pauling Primary School

My Mum

Cuddly as a marshmallow,
My mum's as fast as a car.

My mum's like a cottage - she covers me,
Like a piano, she is always gentle.

My mum's a rose - she is beautiful.
My mum's a cat - she is nice and kind.

My mum's a ruby - gentle
But she can be hot.

Elsie Constantinides (8)
Edward Pauling Primary School

My Mum

My mum is like mashed potato,
Soft, gentle and kind.

She's like a robin,
Cheerful, friendly and cute.

Always like roses,
Pointy, soft and smells nice.

Made like a mansion,
Loves me, cares for me and pretty.

Flash like a Ferrari,
Fast, cool and looks nice.

Pretty like a flute,
Calm, gentle and good.

Sparkly as a diamond,
Sunny, shiny and bright.

Samantha Cooley (8)
Edward Pauling Primary School

Mum

Her voice is spicy like chilli,
Tall like a jeep, big and blonde,
Gigantic and loud like a drum,
Tall like a hollow tree,
Works hard like a beaver,
Like a cottage, big and strong,
A diamond, nice and peaceful.

Jake Cumming (8)
Edward Pauling Primary School

Fudge Is Nuts

Fudge is a nut,
Small, hard and crazy.

The hamster is Formula One,
Fast, cool and noisy.

Like a hotel she is always,
Annoying, hungry and busy.

Sometimes she is Mozart, nice and calm,
Or as loud as scratching.

She is like a butterfly,
Soft, colourful and light.

She is an amethyst,
Shiny, beautiful and sweet.

Talal Mussa (9)
Edward Pauling Primary School

Naomi's Uncle

My uncle is a heart going on and on forever,
And ruby hot and fiery like rap,
A bluebell in the forest,
As harmless as a cat,
An ice lolly melting in the sun.

Naomi Lloyd-Barling (9)
Edward Pauling Primary School

Buster - The Great Cat

Buster is like a library,
Calm inside his heart.

Gentle like a marshmallow,
As calm as a mediator.

As sweet as a cuddly toy,
Can't be fierce.

He can be as fast as a F1 car,
Doesn't bite or scratch.

Just like a hotel,
As good as a diamond.

As soft as rose petals,
Buster - the great cat!

Max Brown (9)
Edward Pauling Primary School

The Carnival

The music got louder as I entered
The street of the carnival.
The colourful clothes glittered in the light.

The people sang like birds,
I couldn't believe I was there,
I wished that I could sing and
Dance as well as them,
I was so amazed by the things I saw.

Everyone was dancing and joining in,
So I decided to dance and join in too.
I was so happy,
It was my dream come true!

Tracy Tandoh (11)
Edward Pauling Primary School

My Mum

My mum is like a pineapple,
Sweet inside and spiky outside.

Always calm and gentle,
Like Mozart in my ears.

My mum shines like a diamond,
Sparkling through the night.

Sometimes shouts like a dog,
When they bark and screech.

Like a theatre, loud and big,
Very cheerful and always kind.

Sometimes sings softly and calmly,
Just like a bird that tweets.

Jodie Harding (9)
Edward Pauling Primary School

My Fairy

My fairy
Is beautiful.
She has a
Big wand.
It sparkles in the dark.
She has huge wings
That glow in the dark.
My fairy has a pair of pink shoes.
My fairy is the best.

Mia Matthews (8)
Laleham CE Primary School

Winter Poem

On Monday I smelt fresh flowers,
Then I saw smoke coming out of the towers.

On Tuesday I saw a flash of lightning,
After there was quite a lot of fighting.

On Wednesday I heard Santa's sleigh jingle,
It made my spine sit up and tingle.

On Thursday I touched a prickly pine cone,
Then I ran as fast as I could back home.

On Friday I tasted bacon and eggs,
Then I played with my mother's pegs.

Maddie Payne (7)
Laleham CE Primary School

Winter Poem

On Monday morning I woke up and smelt the roast meat,
I was so surprised that I fell to my feet.

On Tuesday night I heard thunder and rain,
With a hard pain, what a shame!

On Wednesday morning I had a pet cat,
And it's always on the mat.

On Thursday night, I saw some snowflakes,
So I went to the lake.

Connie Boughey (7)
Laleham CE Primary School

Shape Poem

Apples are delicious,
They make your teeth go green,
They are so scrummy and so yummy,
It makes me funny in my tummy,
Green and green, it is my favourite colour,
They are really delicious but very juicy,
They are my favourite fruit.

Matthew Birt (8)
Laleham CE Primary School

Shape Poem

Bunnies have
Fluffy tails,
Glossy ears
And long,
White, thick
Noses. They are
Very fluffy.

Megan Bredo (7)
Laleham CE Primary School

Shape Poem

Fish are round
Fish are all different colours,
Fish are fat,
Fish are hard to catch,
Fish are all shapes and sizes,
Fish are all different colours.

Alisha Brittany Rulton (8)
Laleham CE Primary School

The Snowy Week

Monday I woke up and went to my car,
The snow had fallen wide and far.

Tuesday I felt the snow in my boot,
My music teacher taught me how to play
Merry Christmas on the flute.

Wednesday I was walking, some snow went in my hair,
All my friends laughed at me but I didn't care.

Thursday I made angels when I went out to play,
I had a good time, that snowy day.

Friday I saw a robin making his nest,
It was so cold, I had to wear a vest.

Elloise Matthews (7)
Laleham CE Primary School

My Annoying Sister

What I hate about my sister
Is whenever I score a goal she boos.

What I like about my sister
Is she looks up to me.

What I hate about my sister
Is she always says we can't watch football.

What I like about my sister
Is she plays with me.

What I hate about my sister
Is that she's mean to me.

Christian Collins (8)
Laleham CE Primary School

Like/Hate Poem

I hate my brother because
He never lets me in his room.

What I like about my brother
Is he lets me watch my TV.

What I hate about my brother
Is he screams like a one year old.

What I like about my brother
Is he makes me laugh.

What I hate about my brother
Is when he punches me.

What I like about my brother
Is when he lets me on his scooter.

Lewis Ridley (8)
Laleham CE Primary School

Like/Hate Poem

What I hate about my brother
Is he always annoys me.

What I like about my brother
Is he always plays the PlayStation with me.

What I hate about my brother
Is he sometimes wakes me up.

What I like about my brother
Is he waits for me to play football with him.

What I hate about my brother
Is that he sometimes hurts me.

What I like about my brother
Is that he plays fairly with me.

Matthew Cooper (7)
Laleham CE Primary School

A Winter's Weekend

On Monday I saw one, big snowman,
In one he had a frying pan.

On Tuesday, it was soggy and cold and I felt so tired and old.

On Wednesday, I smelt mince pies when the air was very dry.

On Thursday, I heard the hot crackling fire with all the people
Singing in the choir.

On Friday, I felt chilly and damp with a very big lamp.

Emily Jaye (8)
Laleham CE Primary School

Shape Poem

I love fish
And so do you.
There are big fish and
There are little fish
Swimming around.
They are in the sea,
And in the river.

Natasha Znetyniak (8)
Laleham CE Primary School

Fire And Water

The fire is blazing in my veins
There are loads of pains
Coming and making me fear
I can't even hear.

The water was full of ice
It was a taste of spice
And very cool
And was like a swimming pool.

Reece Narang (9)
St John Fisher RC Primary School, Perivale, Greenford

Happily Ever After

King Arthur, he's the man
If he can't do it no one can.
He fought bossy barons,
Breathtaking beasts, his motto is:
One for all and all for me!

Lancelot, the bold and brave
Stepped into a dragon's cave.
He was as frightened as a bug,
All he needed was a big hug
But no! He went and slain it for all,
That's why I saw him at the mall!

Gwain, the very strange and silly
Got married to an ugly old bat. What a silly Billy.
One day she turned pretty but forgot her name,
Yet she stole all the fame!

The black knight, he's a scare,
That's why no one voted him mayor!
Creepy as the dead of night,
He never goes in the light.
What a shame! With all his might!

Oh lady Guinevere, you're so pretty
Golden eyes as bright as the moon
Her hair turns brown at the strike of noon,
She got married to King Arthur!
Everyone lived happily ever after!

Louise Charles (9)
St John Fisher RC Primary School, Perivale, Greenford

The Water's Way

The raging rapids
Are like
Rampaging rogue rhinos.

The wicked whirlpools
Whip mighty sailors
Into rocks.

The sliding stream
Is as slippery as an
Electric eel.

The stormy sea
Would sink any ship
And would strike away
The moon and stars.

The terrible tsunami
Put paradise down to
The sea.

The atomic oceans
Have drowned people of power,
But are home to the underwater world.

The great and mighty waterfalls
Are the size of whales
And with a *crash* they kill everything.

Nathan Byrne (9)
St John Fisher RC Primary School, Perivale, Greenford

A Traditional Tale

A spooky and terrifying sight,
Black and petrifying to look at,
It moves silently, but sternly,
In an enchanted forest.

He is brave,
But all alone,
In a horrible, slimy, steaming battlefield.
No lights.
A black knight.

Is he alone? A sound of footsteps,
He listens carefully,
As blind as a bat.
No one still.

Suddenly,
The swish of a sword,
The midnight howling in the distance.
Someone is with him.

He is terrified,
But enough courage to listen,
He has never been defeated.
This is his territory.

He has come across many fierce warriors,
Everyone, now his victim.
His powerful armour can never be damaged,
Until now, maybe?

The creature dives forward,
Crunching on bones,
It dives, he ducks.
It's missed.

He twirls his shiny sword,
Just once,
Crash! Bang!
The creature's dead.

Nothing or anyone can defeat him.
Queen Guinevere, light and lovely,
Great and glorious,
Worships him.

Her eyes are a shiny glance,
Putting the black knight in a trance,
Walking on glory, love and laughter,
They both live happily ever after.

Stefan Browne (10)
St John Fisher RC Primary School, Perivale, Greenford

Happiness

Happiness is like a rainbow,
In the sky for all to see.
It's like children playing in a park,
It's as beautiful as daffodils and tulips,
Growing slowly in the fields.
Happiness sounds like laughter,
From everyone in the world.
Happiness feels like something warm,
Bubbling inside your heart.
Happiness smells like a thousand red roses,
Made into a bouquet especially for you.
Happiness looks like a beautiful butterfly,
That landed on your finger.
Happiness tastes like a marvellous chocolate cake,
That you can eat all by yourself.
Happiness reminds me of the summer holidays,
And rainbows that look like colourful ribbons in the sky.
Happiness is the best thing in the world for me.

Anna Maria Dziedzic (9)
St John Fisher RC Primary School, Perivale, Greenford

Happy Is The Opposite Of Sad

Happy is nice like a calm cat
Happy is a bright yellow beaming sun
Happy is a purr of a cuddly, cute kitten
Happy is like a puppy's soft fur
Happy smells like rich, sweet chocolate
Happy reminds me of my dog, Snoopy
I love to be happy.
The opposite of happy is sad.

Sad is upsetting like losing your family
Sad is dark blue like the massive ocean
Sad sounds like the screech of someone dying
Sad feels like your friend is ill
Sad smells like dark, rotten blood
Sad looks like a dead person
Sad reminds me of my lost dog and dead rabbit
I hate to be sad.

Conor Coules (9)
St John Fisher RC Primary School, Perivale, Greenford

My Special Place

This special setting is the place for me.
Roses bright red, reminding me of bed.
Everything seems slow, under the sun.
Brightness is everywhere, life has begun.

Everything is peaceful, smooth,
Like leaves on a tree on a calm summer's day.
The deer, rabbits and squirrels too
Everything is elegant, makes me so intelligent.

When night comes around, colour will fade,
But my beautiful memory has already been made.
What a beautiful place, just like paradise.
Can you guess where it is?

Joy Tshiala (9)
St John Fisher RC Primary School, Perivale, Greenford

Anger

Anger is as red as fire
It sounds like a terrible, thundery storm.

It feels like a hard stone
Lying on a seashore, all alone.

Raging anger reminds me of popping!
Like a balloon which has been blown up
So forcefully, it pops!

Anger is a screaming, screeching noise.
Echoes through my ears, causing many tears.

Anger sounds like a roaring lion.
It smells foul, like a slowly rotting vegetable.

Lingering all around, like arching cobwebs,
A rainbow would be a nicer arch.
What do you think?

Ramsey Badir (10)
St John Fisher RC Primary School, Perivale, Greenford

The Wonderful Laughter

Laughter is a big red balloon!
It stretches around my friends and family.
It tastes as sweet as a delicious, delightful strawberry.

It sounds like a wonderful choir,
Chanting sweet hymns at Christmas time.
It feels like a fluffy, soft pillow lying on a bed of rose petals.

It smells like a rose garden
And looks like a lovely Easter lily and most importantly,
Reminds me of a lovely, cheerful summer's day!

I love seeing and hearing laughter!

Rebecca Amy Kelleher (10)
St John Fisher RC Primary School, Perivale, Greenford

The Prince And The Forest

The forest is green,
Like runner beans,
It sounds like a whistle,
In the breeze
People walk by and always say,
'What a peaceful forest behind that hedge.'

Now a prince rides by and screams,
'I must show my father what a nice forest this seems.'
The next day, guess what he saw?
Lots of animals shaking paws.

The forest turned to a rainbow,
Because of the animals.
He shouted, 'Get away from the peaceful forest.'

All was quiet once again,
Thanks to the prince for making it tame.

Richard Williams (9)
St John Fisher RC Primary School, Perivale, Greenford

The Poor Man

The waves were as fast as thrashing speed.
It was too fast, I could not read.
I sat along the windy water,
It was magical and full of excitement.

Splash went the waves,
Someone fell in.
I could not help it,
I have to save him.

I rushed and ran
To save the poor man,
I just did not know what to do!

Maryam Ali (9)
St John Fisher RC Primary School, Perivale, Greenford

Sweet Forest

The enchanted forest is as green as lime,
It's so calm and peaceful; I could stay there all day,
With birds singing sweet tunes every day
So all I can hear are the sweet sounds of nature.

The enchanted forest feels so relaxing, calm and peaceful,
That it is the only dream that could come true.
With the trees and bushes green as green could be,
It feels like you're floating up to Heaven.

The enchanted forest is so refreshing,
With ever so sweet smells as if a sweet smelling candle
Has been burning for years
The smell is so sweet I can imagine a huge flower.

It looks so, so neat, tidy and will never get a spot of dirt,
With neat nests built in tall trees and birds
With spotless, shiny, bright beaks
And right behind the enchanted forest
Is the sun gleaming with all its power and might.

Now it's nearly the end of the day
With the sunset ever so colourful.
With the darkness covering the light,
Then the sun goes down and the stars appear,
But now it's time for time to go, so *bye!*

Anrika Thinju (9)
St John Fisher RC Primary School, Perivale, Greenford

Different Waters

Water is the colour of blue,
It can be foggy and it can be clear,
Sometimes it is transparent too,
Like when water is drank by a deer.

It is rampaging and fierce when at sea,
The water is a volcano exploding rocket-like,
And it's not just coming from me,
Because at times it is as sharp as a spike!

You can swim in the water any time,
Either hot, cold or warm,
It is made into a drink of water and lime
And in a bottle it is a water swarm!

We need water to live,
For it has good stuff inside,
Shaking us with water like a super, stupid sieve,
Because don't all of us like to still be alive?

Water tastes like nothing in fact,
Just boring and simple, just like that!
Like invisible people dancing in liquid doing an act,
As silent as a sleeping cat.

Water is used for many things,
Rivers, lakes and seas,
Water is obviously used by queens and kings,
So you could go to the River Thames
To collect water without any fees!

Laurel Dunne (9)
St John Fisher RC Primary School, Perivale, Greenford

The Frightening Black Knight

The black knight is so ferocious,
He goes out in the night, his face flashing fright.

His intention is to slay, anyone who comes in sight,
He is terrified of daylight.

He will come and bite you if you turn on your light,
His horse is called Lightning Strike.

Pulling out his sword like a strike of lightning,
It glistens and gleams, oh how fascinating!

Galloping on his horse like roaring thunder,
Scary and fierce, the world is his oyster.

Only to be encountered on a bony battlefield,
Beware! He will scare!

Only if you dare!

Darnell Noel (10)
St John Fisher RC Primary School, Perivale, Greenford

Fire

My eyes turned into fire,
My heart turned as black as the misty sky,
My chest was filled with fire,
I felt evil.

My eyes were red balls of raging fire,
My face turned redder than Mars,
My fist clenched as my eyes were on fire.

The soft and calm dropped out of me
And the anger overlapped me.
All of a sudden I became a devil for eternal life,
It made me feel hotter than a lump of fire.

Suzy Hermiz (10)
St John Fisher RC Primary School, Perivale, Greenford

Spooky, Scary Forest

A scary forest
is not the place for me,
it really gives me the creeps
and is very deep,
rough as a pavement, tall as a tree,
I will never go there, it was just you and me.

My friend told me to go in there,
I can't believe I took that dare,
all I wanted to do was go to bed.

But then I bumped my head,
this was the worst day ever,
then I saw a piece of leather
I wondered where it came from.

I saw something quick,
It was as quick as a shooting star in the sky.
I was so hungry, my mum was making my favourite pie.
I just wanted to go home and be alone.

So I turned around and went back home to bed,
still with the bump on my head.

Alison Gayle (10)
St John Fisher RC Primary School, Perivale, Greenford

Weather

In the forest the wind is whooshing, puddles splashing,
Droplets clashing and thunder gushing.
The forest's dark and green and leaves are crunching.
The mud's like a swamp trying to suck you in.
The nasty branches try to hit you in the face as you walk along.
The rain tries to wet you as you walk along
But at last the storm has stopped. *Hooray!*

Daniel Kucharski (9)
St John Fisher RC Primary School, Perivale, Greenford

King Arthur

King Arthur,
with his shiny, silver sword,
challenges fierce dragons,
as big as elephants,
all as tall as towers.
He would challenge any creature,
big or small.

Sir Gawain is as brave as a lion,
as fast as a cheetah
looking for his prey.
If you want to win a battle,
look no further!

The brilliant black knight,
may give you a fright,
night recognisable in the darkness,
never ventures in his battleground!

All fight for the kingdom,
which one should deserve it?
The ugly lady is watching,
she plans to present it.

Reem Gubbawy (10)
St John Fisher RC Primary School, Perivale, Greenford

Excalibur

Excalibur, Excalibur my fair sword
You are so powerful, your handle is pure gold
And your blade is a sharp sword.
Cling! Clank!
Your blade is a feather.
You're the greatest in the world.
I want you as my weapon.
Blood in the air
You're the best so let me have you please.

Patrick David (10)
St John Fisher RC Primary School, Perivale, Greenford

Fierce Cyclops

This meat-eating, giant Cyclops is ten feet tall.
His horn is as sharp as a butcher's knife.
He is a treacherous beast
And you might be his next feast.

And if you go to his lair
He'll embrace you with his stare!
I've heard many tales
Of monstrous acts he's committed,
Believe me he's one not to be acquitted.

He screams and growls
And it echoes through the land
Like the music of jazz musicians
Playing in a band.

His face reminds me of bubbling clay,
Wrinkly and rough, ready to decay!
My advice to you is sleep tight
Or you might get a fright.

So leave this Greek monster alone.
On one will take his throne!

Christopher Makar (10)
St John Fisher RC Primary School, Perivale, Greenford

Anger

The anger was violent and as red as blood.
Burning fire was as red as the fist.
Bones were sticking out of the bloodstream.
Blood of anger shot like a fireball
But beware the thunder ball might be there.
The eyes were raging balls of fire.
You will have to take care.

Jade O'Rourke (9)
St John Fisher RC Primary School, Perivale, Greenford

The Black Knight

The black knight is an evil man,
He will give you a big fright, but always at night,
Because he's scared of daylight.

The black knight is a deadly man,
He will challenge you whenever he can.
If you try to fight him, you will never beat or defeat him.

The black knight is a sad and lonely man,
He never lets anyone be his friend,
Each time someone tries, he stares with his evil eyes,
Pulls out his sword, then yells and roars,
So no one will be his friend.

The black knight whips out his sword in bravery,
Towering tall above all other knights,
His presence is felt by everyone around,
Will he soon again be crowned?

The black knight is an evil man.

Sterling Record (10)
St John Fisher RC Primary School, Perivale, Greenford

The Fire And Anger

The fire is frustrating and the anger is mad
It is so powerful that it's like a thousand bombs banging.
The anger is a sign of someone angry inside.
The anger and fire mix to make an angry, fire-breathing person.
The face of it is a fireball face.
The hot flame-like volcano is a dangerous volcano
Because it popped out the bubble and flew up in the air.
The fire is a sign
The angry fire-breathing person lies in the dangerous volcano.

Liam Nee (10)
St John Fisher RC Primary School, Perivale, Greenford

My Little Sister

My little sister
Likes swapping her things
And she always plays on the swings

She can be annoying sometimes
And she thinks she can say her rhymes
So I clap from behind

When my sister tells me off
I get very angry
And volcanoes are erupting in me

I also feel sharp red fire in me,
But that's how I will be

She always tells on me
And if you hear my mum shout
That's where I will be.

Rebecca Okine (10)
St John Fisher RC Primary School, Perivale, Greenford

Thunder And Lightning

Bang, tear, crash,
This is the sound everybody fears.
Thick thunder thrashes and lightning bashes
The explosion puts fear in the hearts of everyone.

After it strikes all that's left is small scorch marks
Everyone feels fear in their hearts.
Everybody knows it's coming when they hear dogs bark
People are frightened and they should be.

People feel joyful, but then comes the sound
Everybody cries.
Everyone kisses his or her lucky pound
As soon as you're hit you will disappear.

Liam Mannion (10)
St John Fisher RC Primary School, Perivale, Greenford

King Arthur

King Arthur and his knights
Were always filled with might
They carried shiny swords
And never betrayed their lord

The king went up against the black knight
A petrifying laugh filled the darkened, airless night
He was scared to death but yet he had courage to listen
The black knight's armour glistened

King Arthur had a wife
The shining jewel in his life
Guinevere was her name
The one whose love prevailed
King Arthur was in a trance
With one shining glance

Merlin, King Arthur's wizard was wise but old
He could cook up blizzards icy cold
His kind glistening eyes were magic
Unfortunately his death was tragic.

Till the day of King Arthur's death
He had trust, love, loyalty and wealth
That is the poem of King Arthur's life
With Merlin, his knights and his loving wife.

Kathrine Tyler (9)
St John Fisher RC Primary School, Perivale, Greenford

My Poem

A caress of wind on my calm face
A lot of people splashing together in the light blue sea
A soft sound of birds singing and singing
A kiss of sunshine on my beautiful face
A beautiful breeze on my hot face.

Christina Symeon (8)
St John Fisher RC Primary School, Perivale, Greenford

Water

The ocean of relaxation was as calm as ice,
Never tough, never strong, never furious.
It was motionless and everyone found it nice
Smooth and cool, never powerful.

The ocean of waves crashes against the shore,
The ocean glistens like diamonds
And everyone who goes there is never poor,
Strong and tough is this ocean.

The ocean of fury is rough and deadly,
The ocean is black and eerie,
Rapid, cruel and feels like death is in the air
Very scary.

Rianna Wright Macleod (9)
St John Fisher RC Primary School, Perivale, Greenford

Stormy

The stormy, thundering lightning,
Crashed upon the deep blue sea.
It was so destructive
That anyone who went near it had to flee.

The furious fuming twister
Was as wrathful as a beast.
It never set to rest,
Because it needed its daily feast.

It sounds like *crash, bang, wallop!*
When it's really mad.
It looks like a scary monster
And it's extremely bad.

Charlie Wright (10)
St John Fisher RC Primary School, Perivale, Greenford

Fire

Fire is a blazing hot ball that burns your hands
When I'm mad I know the Devil is with me.
My heart is red like fireworks shooting up.
It smells like hot chillies in a pot,
Like a volcano,
The lava bubbles come up,
Like water boiling in a saucepan
Bubble! Bubble! Bubble!
Steam is coming out of my ears that is black,
Swiiich.

Fire burning the wood for light,
It makes a bright flame dance
In the darkness,
Flowing side to side.
It reminds me of Hades,
Madness is in the air.
Swiiich.

Fire burning, killing people,
It's dangerous so be aware.
Volcanoes bursting up,
Like a cannonball in the air,
Dragons breathing the knights to death.
Swiiich.

Domini Lovesey (10)
St John Fisher RC Primary School, Perivale, Greenford

A Windy Day

A windy breeze coming towards me
A slap of wind falling on me
A nervous feeling going away
A noisy sound - dogs barking
A miserable feeling of wind.

Sara-Louise Tawfig (9)
St John Fisher RC Primary School, Perivale, Greenford

Water Poem

The deep blue ocean shimmered
On the blazing, burning sun.
Paradise was warm, calm and
Seaweed slid to the shore.

Everything was quiet
Everything sparkled.

Bang, clink, woo

The ocean's waves became a roaring lion.

The water blasted past the deep, soft, sliding sand.
It was chaos, the water became furious.

The ocean became bland, grey and gloomy,

The wind was like a lion, it became cold then it
Became very rough and violent.

Jessica Tiongson (10)
St John Fisher RC Primary School, Perivale, Greenford

The Very Stormy Day

Once there was a storm
Which made my eyes red as fire.
When my eyes were like fire,
I felt like there was a twister
Burning in my hands.
I felt like my head was going to blow
Like a fireball.
So I turned around
And I looked up at the very stormy sky
And saw red fireballs
Made out of big, big rocks,
Which were coming at me
And making my body as black as the sky.
Suddenly, a few minutes later,
The storm stopped.

Sarah Ishak (9)
St John Fisher RC Primary School, Perivale, Greenford

The Slightly Salty Sea

The sea is very, very salty,
It is sour, actually quite malty.
When you put your feet in it, it tickles your toes,
Whilst the air, it brushes against your nose.
If you bathe in it, you might float,
But if you look far away from shore,
You might see a boat.
You feel like you don't have a care in the world
And then the waves turn swirled.
Then it comes to the end of the day,
So there is no one there to play.
When it is a brand new day,
The sea is as if it was underneath a big tray.
Swoosh, swoosh, swoosh, go the mollified waves,
Seeing as they reflect on them,
The sun's rays are their slaves.

Maisy Ginnelly (9)
St John Fisher RC Primary School, Perivale, Greenford

Excalibur

Excalibur, Excalibur, will you slay this beast?
And I shall give you a feast, a feast.
The sound of you, clash and destroy the creature
Makes you a really big feature, a feature.
I love the shine on you when the fire is cut
And when the battle is won I shall clean you in the sun.
The mirror is like the sword, it reflects the fire,
As the fire is burning the life of the knight.

The fire of the world is burning in my soul.
If the fire was underground the life of the mole is gone.
The fire will crash into my house and destroy it.
My house will turn into lava and it will be gone if the battle is lost.
If it is won I will have a house plus two buns!

Shane Carville (10)
St John Fisher RC Primary School, Perivale, Greenford

The Wave Of Death

The wave of death crashes
Like ten thousand bombs
It carries lots of strength
Think nothing can stand in its way
The mighty Excalibur thrusts its power
But still it keeps coming.

The knights ran away like mad chickens
If you touch them, they push you miles away.
It is the toughest, meanest thing
That has ever happened.
Everything that is happening now is bad.
The world is in great danger.

The scientists are trying to stop it
Or do something about it.
But they don't know how.
They are trying to build a machine to stop it.
Everyone is praying for mercy,
But it keeps on coming.

Cedric Eid (9)
St John Fisher RC Primary School, Perivale, Greenford

A Patch Of Rain

Heaps of rain falling down,
There is no beautiful sun around,
People are running to their wet cars,
Miserable weather go away!
We will let you come back
Another horrible day . . . maybe!

Georgia Corr (8)
St John Fisher RC Primary School, Perivale, Greenford

Sunny Summer Days!

People sunbathing, going for fun to the exciting beach
to swim and cool themselves down.
The warmth of the sunny sun is on my smooth, shiny face.
A soft breeze passes by.
The sweet scent of the shimmering water
swishing by, nothing can bother you
now that you are resting peacefully.
When you get too hot then you dive underwater
and feel all the different types of wiggly, swimming fishes
and if they like you, they may even tickle you.
Walking on the glittery sand, making sandcastles.
Swoosh! The water takes it away.
Going back into the water,
A big wave is coming,
a big hand scoops you up carefully
and returns you to the glimmering shore.

Dana Sousa-Limbu (8)
St John Fisher RC Primary School, Perivale, Greenford

Yellow Sun

A beautiful sun in the blue sky,
A sparkling ocean all around my eyes
Wonderful golden sand on top of the land,
A refreshing smell in the blue sky,
A cool wind near my pool,
An awesome horizon all around.

Allaan Heewa (8)
St John Fisher RC Primary School, Perivale, Greenford

The 7th May: A Very Sunny Day

The 7th May: a very sunny day
with the birds singing in the trees,
butterflies beautifully swooping through the air
and dogs barking happily in the park.
The barbecue on and the big paddling pool out.
There are also many people on holiday.
Outside the sky is very clear,
there are no dark clouds
and the sun is shining brightly.
The 7th May: a sunny day but don't forget to have *fun!*

Vikki Newbert (8)
St John Fisher RC Primary School, Perivale, Greenford

Sunny Days

Birds come out and sing,
People go to the park,
They smell of sweet flowers.
Children come out to play,
Singing 'Hooray! Hooray!
School's over, let's play.'

Antony El-Nawar (9)
St John Fisher RC Primary School, Perivale, Greenford

Summer For All To Share

The flowers start blooming,
Summer is here,
Sweet birds are singing sweetly,
Summer is here.

Aaron Walker (8)
St John Fisher RC Primary School, Perivale, Greenford

Winter Wonders

A flake of snow
fell down from the sky
and a powerful gust of wind
whirled around forcefully
with the snow.
The grass is frosty
and it's so white
and so bright.
A pinch of cold
is pulling me back.

Edward Deeney (9)
St John Fisher RC Primary School, Perivale, Greenford

Rainy Beach

Hard drops of icy water in the sea
Waves attacking from the deep
Dolphins trying to get away
Sharks celebrating with hunger
People too scared to go into the most
Dangerous sea.
The nature never ends . . .

Joanna Rudzka (9)
St John Fisher RC Primary School, Perivale, Greenford

Snowy Scotland

A slap of snow, a touch of sleet,
A snowball in the eye, an icy path.
A pinch of cold pulling me back,
A punch of freezing wind floating by my face.
Two big heavy boots trying to walk,
Solid and heavy rain.

Alice Starrs (9)
St John Fisher RC Primary School, Perivale, Greenford

Yellow Sunshine

A gentle kiss of warm sunshine on my fresh face,
A soft touch of magical wind on my back,
An excited sweet feeling of going out the door,
A lovely sound of beautiful birds,
A warm, nice feeling of summertime.

Jordan White (9)
St John Fisher RC Primary School, Perivale, Greenford

Wintry Days

One snowy Christmas Day people were snowboarding
On the pure white snow
People were throwing snowballs at each other
People were making snowmen
People were making big snowballs.

Bessan Awezie (9)
St John Fisher RC Primary School, Perivale, Greenford

Sunny Outing In The Sun

A gentle kiss of sunshine on my face,
Sun cream on my beautiful light skin,
Sun shining as hot sunshine,
Sun shining like a hot crab,
Sunny crabs excited to pinch,
Nice calm children swimming in hot sea.
Sun bright, bright sun.

Rahelan Ujayakamar (8)
St John Fisher RC Primary School, Perivale, Greenford

Summer

Summer is golden, blue and green,
It tastes like pizza and ice cream,
It sounds like sports day and swimming,
It looks like boats bobbing in the sea,
It smells like perfumed roses,
It makes me feel happy and relaxed.

Kajani Subhaskaran (7)
St John Fisher RC Primary School, Perivale, Greenford

Snowy Days

Snowflakes falling slowly and gently,
Snowballs flying all over the place,
Snow covering the car and the back garden.
Snow, how beautiful you are, how I love you,
People making snowmen.

Joshua Mendonca (8)
St John Fisher RC Primary School, Perivale, Greenford

The Candle Flame

The candle flame is shining like the evening star,
The candle flame is shivering like the ice cream melting,
The candle flame is darting like a rocket,
The candle flame is spitting like a sweet candle,
The candle flame is leaping like an excited child.

Conor Tynan (7)
St John Fisher RC Primary School, Perivale, Greenford

A Poem To Be Spoken Silently

(Based on 'A Poem To Be Spoken Silently' by Pie Corbett)

It was so silent that I heard the front door unlock
like leaves falling off a tree . . .

It was so peaceful that I heard an ant crawling across the playground
like a plastic bag rustling . . .

It was so still that I felt a raindrop
as it was dropping on the window as it tickled the windowpane . . .

It was so silent that I heard the mouse for the computer click,
'I feel lonely . . .'

It was so quiet that I heard
a tooth come out of Jon's mouth.

It was so hushed that I heard
a spider walking around its web.

Sinead Douglas (8)
St John Fisher RC Primary School, Perivale, Greenford

Christmas

Christmas is white, dark blue and crystal clear.
It looks like a snowman, Jesus and Christmas trees,
also, it looks like holly and bobbles.
Christmas tastes like roast turkey,
mashed potato, hot chocolate and green beans.
Christmas sounds like bashing snowballs,
quiet, gentle and very peaceful.
Christmas smells like roast turkey,
pine leaves, cinnamon and perfumed candles.
Christmas makes me feel cold, happy,
joyful and most of all, *excited.*

Aoife McGovern (7)
St John Fisher RC Primary School, Perivale, Greenford

Summer

Summer is a big, yellow sun, and salty beach water,
It tastes like juicy watermelons and yummy pies,
It sounds like birds chirping,
It looks like dolphins jumping and a ship sailing,
It smells like lovely hot dogs,
It makes me feel free and relaxed.

Mithun Arun Kumaran (7)
St John Fisher RC Primary School, Perivale, Greenford

Christmas

Christmas is white
It makes me feel happy
It smells fresh
It tastes like soup and hot chocolate
It sounds peaceful
It looks fun.

Ciera Walsh (8)
St John Fisher RC Primary School, Perivale, Greenford

Autumn

Autumn is bright and colourful,
It tastes like marshmallows,
It sounds like rain falling on the floor,
It looks like different colours of leaves,
It smells like a bunch of banana skins,
It makes me feel so happy.

Jonathan Perera Gunathilaka (7)
St John Fisher RC Primary School, Perivale, Greenford

The Candle Flame

The candle flame
is shining like a
rajah's diamond.

The candle flame
is melting like an
ice cube.

The candle flame
is dancing like a
ballerina.

The candle flame
is glistening like a
disco ball.

The candle flame
is fluttering like a
butterfly's wing.

The candle flame
is wobbling like a
jelly bean.

The candle flame
is shining like the
sun.

The candle flame
is like a light
of the world.

Namir Métë (7)
St John Fisher RC Primary School, Perivale, Greenford

Snow Days

A snowball hits me on my leg,
Children throwing snowballs at others.
Making snowmen and snowballs all day long.
I'm having lots of fun.

Sean Filgate (8)
St John Fisher RC Primary School, Perivale, Greenford

Spring

Spring is a lovely blue sky, a bright yellow sun with pink blossoms,
It tastes like a juicy watermelon and cool cola,
It sounds like singing birds and the first cuckoo,
It looks like jumpy bunnies, cats and fast squirrels,
It smells like new life and fresh daffodils,
It makes me feel joyful and excited.

Kamila Fiedorczyk (8)
St John Fisher RC Primary School, Perivale, Greenford

A Heart

A heart is a sign of peace and love and joy.
It is lovely and a nice shape,
It is very colourful.
A heart goes *ding bing* like a string,
A heart beats fast or slow,
A heart is a lovely thing,
A heart shines like a sun, but a red sun!

Preny Hovanessian (7)
St John Fisher RC Primary School, Perivale, Greenford

A Poem To Be Spoken Silently

(Based on 'A Poem To Be Spoken Silently' by Pie Corbett)

It was so silent that I heard a squeaky mouse,
It was so quiet that I felt like I was flying,
It was so peaceful that I heard a butterfly,
It was so still that I heard a strange noise,
It was so hushed that I heard a strange noise,
It was so hushed that I heard a car.

Nicole Louro Serrano (7)
St John Fisher RC Primary School, Perivale, Greenford

A Poem To Be Spoken Silently

(Based on 'A Poem To Be Spoken Silently' by Pie Corbett)

It was so silent that I could hear
a caterpillar crawling on a branch of a tree
like a butterfly fluttering its wings.

It was so peaceful I could hear
a bird flying in the air
like my teacher writing on the board.

It was so still I could feel
a snowflake falling on the ground
just like an angel coming down from the sky.

It was so silent that I could hear
my blood running through my body
like a mouse running to his house
so he wouldn't be eaten by the cat.

Amy Ryan (7)
St John Fisher RC Primary School, Perivale, Greenford

The Candle Flame

The candle flame
dances like a swan.

The candle flame
shines like the evening star.

The candle flame
flickers like a huge fire.

The candle flame
shakes like it is so cold.

The candle flame
is wiggling like a pop star.

Connor Burden (8)
St John Fisher RC Primary School, Perivale, Greenford

A Poem To Be Spoken Silently

(Based on 'A Poem To Be Spoken Silently' by Pie Corbett)

It was so silent that I heard
a leaf fall to the ground
like a feather from my pillow . . .

I heard an ant crawling round
and round in circles,
chasing his friend and scattering out the door.

I heard a rustle
in the trees
outside the window.

It was so quiet
that I heard
a little robin jump.

It was so quiet
that I heard
a spider crawl on a stick.

Karalo Dunne (7)
St John Fisher RC Primary School, Perivale, Greenford

The Candle Flame

The candle flame
is wiggling like jelly.

The candle flame
is leaping like a silly frog.

The candle flame
is dripping like water.

The candle flame
is shining like a rajah's diadem.

The candle flame
is sparkling like the star on Christmas Night.

Joseph Sheehan (8)
St John Fisher RC Primary School, Perivale, Greenford

The Candle Flame

The candle shines like a diamond,
The candle flame is melting like a landslide.
The candle flame is shaking like an earthquake.
The candle flame is shining like the sun,
The candle flame is boxing with a boxer,
The candle flame is shining like a rajah's diadem,
The candle flame is dancing like a ballerina.

Daniel Siban (8)
St John Fisher RC Primary School, Perivale, Greenford

The Candle Flame

The candle flame leaps like a drop of snow,
The candle flame is glittering like a morning star,
The candle flame is shining like an evening star,
The candle flame is like the bright frog,
The candle flame is like a shimmering disco ball,
The candle flame is like a melting ballerina.

David Golesz (8)
St John Fisher RC Primary School, Perivale, Greenford

Autumn

Autumn and dark grey
It tastes like bread for supper,
It sounds like leaves falling,
It looks like a bonfire,
It makes me feel happy.

Martyna Rybakowska (7)
St John Fisher RC Primary School, Perivale, Greenford

The Spooky Poem

(Based on 'A Poem To Be Spoken Silently' by Pie Corbett)

It was so silent that I heard a pin drop on the ground,
It was so quiet that I felt a ladybird crawling up on my hand,
It was so peaceful that I heard a snowflake drop to the ground,
It was so still I heard a spider making its web.
It was so hushed that I heard a bee biting someone.

Tonya Likosso (8)
St John Fisher RC Primary School, Perivale, Greenford

I Dream Of My Country

I miss my country ever so much,
Every minute of my life I think about it.
Even when I am happy there's a sad touch,
My country is like a light that's just been lit,
Showering me with its might.
It's like a sun that has just woken up,
The mysterious mountains hold me tight.

My country is a big secret,
It's like it doesn't even exist.
But I know it's something I won't forget,
It's on the top of my favourite list.
I've got so many memories,
Especially when I fell into a lump of berries.
My country doesn't have a big area,
I'll tell you the name, it's Bulgaria!

Chanel Viegas (10)
St Teresa's RC First & Middle School, Harrow Weald

My Sisters

My smallest sister, Charlotte
Is very cheeky.
Charlotte is an annoying little devil.
She is like a monkey in a case.

My oldest sister, Laura
Is very loud.
Laura is very lucky,
She wins all the games.
She is like a lion walking around.

Sarah, the one younger than me
Is like a monkey in a tree
Throwing bananas at me.

The second youngest, Emily
Is a devil
Looking at me,
Casting a spell on me.

Without them where would I be?

Karen Street (11)
St Teresa's RC First & Middle School, Harrow Weald

Sausages

Sausages are yummy!
It's better than being funny,
It's better than having a bunny,
It's better than finding a dummy,
Sausages are yummy!
They're good in your tummy,
They're as good as your mummy,
They're as good as honey,
Sausages are yummy!

Rhys Walsh (11)
St Teresa's RC First & Middle School, Harrow Weald

My Ten Pets

I have ten pets and they've all gone mad,
Even my fish have gone completely bad.
Once I tried stopping them,
I ended up running into my pet-proof den.
I have a dog, a cat, a rat,
But the rat ends up in my mum's feathered hat.

My whole family wouldn't be complete,
Without those little creatures running round your feet.

Hollie Ann Conway (11)
St Teresa's RC First & Middle School, Harrow Weald

Unique Thy Name Is Ryan

I'm happy about being unique
Like a dusty clock being dusted
Like a child excited about going on a sunny holiday,
Like a seed glad about seed dispersal
Like a madman electrified about world domination
Like an echidna escaped from a fire and lucky to still be alive.
I'm happy about being unique.

Ryan Dempsey (11)
St Teresa's RC First & Middle School, Harrow Weald

My Sister Who Sings In The Street

My sister woke up and went into the street,
She started to sing while I nicked her sweets
Then she started to dance to the rhythm and the beat.

My next-door neighbour started to peep,
When my sister fell over she started to weep,
Then she got up and made a cheeky pose
Then she noticed she had broken her nose.

Lewis Dickens (11)
St Teresa's RC First & Middle School, Harrow Weald

Models Of Soldiers

Models of soldiers,
Painted quite recently in my spare time,
Noticeable, tiny and mighty,
Like an ant eating your picnic,
Like a black person in a crowd of white people,
Makes you feel massive,
Like a mountain in the middle of lots of hills,
Models of soldiers,
Reminds us that soldiers can be small and still dangerous,
And tells us we should be careful of soldiers,
We think we're smart,
But we're not so smart around models of soldiers.

James Fernandes-Pettingill (10)
St Teresa's RC First & Middle School, Harrow Weald

Rainbows

Red is the colour of a red juicy apple
That grows on a tree.
Orange is the colour of the fat cat, Garfield,
Who fills us all with glee.
Yellow is the colour of the sun,
Gleaming on our world.
Green is the colour of grass
And someone who has just hurled!
Blue is the colour of the ocean
Where all the fish live.
Indigo is the colour of your face
When you're angry like my friend, Viv.
Violet is the colour of those flowers,
I personally like them, me.
These colours make a rainbow
That Noah loved to see.

Dominic Halpin (11)
St Teresa's RC First & Middle School, Harrow Weald

Great Egyptians' Curses

Great Egyptians' curses
Done a thousand years ago
Weird, unlucky, might be bad,
It's like something unlucky
It's like something spooky,
It makes me feel ghostly
Like an unearthly person you see all day.
Great Egyptians' curses
Reminds me how unlucky people's lives are.

Stephen May (10)
St Teresa's RC First & Middle School, Harrow Weald

Cat Rap

I have a little cat that likes to rap,
She likes to twirl around the flap.
She dances to the beat while eating meat.
She is the queen of pop,
She never ever stops!
That's the end of my cat rap.

Shiney Rebera (10)
St Teresa's RC First & Middle School, Harrow Weald

My True Home

My true home is far away,
I came to this country one day.
Buildings, houses, a new life for me,
Nicole, Magda, Natalia, Edyta are no longer here.
Names like Nicky, Tara, Gemma, Jessica, Chanel and Megan,
That is what I hear, my new life begins.
New home, new school, new toys, new kids,
I love my new home but Poland I miss!

Jessica Rolewicz (11)
St Teresa's RC First & Middle School, Harrow Weald

My Mad Family!

I woke up this morning and went downstairs,
I found my mum watching 'Three Little Bears'.
She started reciting it in a baby voice,
Then went on the floor and played with some toys.

I went to the kitchen and saw my dad,
He started chasing my nan, shouting, 'Had!'
My little baby cousin got in a mood,
She then got up and started making her own food.

My sister got up and was surprised like me,
So she woke herself up by making coffee.
But she had too much and started going crazy,
Why couldn't she stay just being lazy?

How would you cope with my mad family?

Chloe Galloway (10)
St Teresa's RC First & Middle School, Harrow Weald

Today's The Day

Today's the day of the big test,
I hope I do my best,
Last night I did not have a rest,
Today's the day of the big test.

Today's the day of the big exam,
I thought I could try a scam,
I feel like I have been hit by a ram,
Today's the day of the big exam.

Today's the day of the big SATs,
My tummy feels like it is full of bats,
I feel like tearing all of my mum's hats,
Today's the day of the big SATs.

Antoine Brier (11)
St Teresa's RC First & Middle School, Harrow Weald

Mirror, Mirror On The Wall

Mirror, mirror on the wall,
Just hanging there in the hall.
How lonely you seem,
But then we can redeem.
We'll move you to the studio,
And then you'll always know . . .

We love you to bits, you're so unique,
100 years old and very antique.

Joe Watson (11)
St Teresa's RC First & Middle School, Harrow Weald

My Messy Bedroom

My bedroom
Is really a mess,
Messy, untidy, covered in toys
Like a blown-up toy shop,
Like an elephant in a glass and mugs shop,
It makes me feel untidy,
Like a person who drops things on the floor.
My bedroom
Reminds us to clean up.

Tom Wickham (11)
St Teresa's RC First & Middle School, Harrow Weald

My Family

My family is a treasure to me,
My mum's a diamond that always shines at me.
My dad's a crown that sits upon my head.
My sister is a lazy jewel that always sparkles in bed.
I think I'm the treasure chest keeping everyone safe.
My family is a treasure to me!

Alex Bastian (10)
St Teresa's RC First & Middle School, Harrow Weald

My Crazy Teacher

The way she teaches
Is totally absurd
But when she comes up close
Her booming voice is heard!

'I might just be your teacher
That's what you might think
But I'll send you to the river
And it's sure that you will sink!'

If I tell you more
Do you promise not to tell?
For if I do
It's sure you'll be sent to Hell!

'The way you play at playtime,
Is really hard to tell
If you're playing football
Oh you think it's swell!'

These things about my teacher
Happened just last week
My teacher, my crazy teacher
Is really quite a freak!

Emily Olive (11)
St Teresa's RC First & Middle School, Harrow Weald

My Baby Sister

My baby sister is annoying as can be,
I still love her, you can see,
She is noisy, like me, blatant to see,
She is nothing like you or me,
She is only two years old, beautiful as can be,
I still love her, you can see.

Nathan Ball (11)
St Teresa's RC First & Middle School, Harrow Weald

Myself

I am a little crazy
I'm sorry I cannot help
My friends all say, 'Hey!'
I go into a daze.

How strange for someone 'normal'
I wish I were great,
Greater than you
Greater than all people.

Oh no!
I have to run,
Run to outer space!
I see all the planets,
How do they stay in place?

Oh I wish I knew,
Knew why I am like this,
But,
I, of course,
Must be
One of the Earth's mysteries!

Nicky Geraghty (11)
St Teresa's RC First & Middle School, Harrow Weald

Great Egyptian Gods

Great Egyptian gods
Lived thousands of years ago
Cool, awesome, weird
Like a king or queen
Like someone who can put their hands through the clouds
Like an ant being watched by a human
Great Egyptian gods
Reminds us of what they were like.

Ryan Calder (10)
St Teresa's RC First & Middle School, Harrow Weald

My TV

When I go home I take off my coat,
Go in my room and get the remote.
I push the button ready to go
And flick through the channels looking for a show.
I push number one, but there is nothing good,
I press number two, but it's Robin Hood.
My mum calls me for dinner, but I refuse to go,
I sit on my bed watching the Blue Peter show.
I sneak my chips into my room,
I called my friend and told her to come soon.
Ten minutes later there was a knock at the door,
I told her to come in, but she sits on the floor.
She went home, but I still watched TV,
My mum came in drinking her disgusting tea.
My TV blew up and I went mad,
I sat on my bed, looking so sad.

Tara Rahilly (10)
St Teresa's RC First & Middle School, Harrow Weald

My Love For Arsenal

I love Arsenal so much
Even though they've lost their touch
I know they are so great
I even wish Henry were my mate!

If Arsenal lose the game
I'll be in a lot of shame
Arsenal will win
Even though Robert Pires needs a trim.

I love Arsenal so much!
Oh how I love them such!

Aaron Pearce (11)
St Teresa's RC First & Middle School, Harrow Weald

When Little Sisters Turn Bad!

I have a little sister,
When she is not around I'm glad.
She is on the PS2 all day round,
When little sisters turn bad!

When I don't get her a drink,
She always shouts out, 'Daaaaaaaaad!'
I end up getting her a drink with ice cubes,
When little sisters turn bad!

Whenever I have a friend around,
She seems to get quite mad.
She wails and whinges so my friend goes home,
When little sisters turn bad!

When she terrorises my black cat Smokey,
I do feel a little bit sad.
Smokey looks like a drowning toddler trying to get away,
When little sisters turn bad!

Once she is asleep though,
(Which I wish she always would).
Finally the house is quiet,
When little sisters are sometimes good!

Rebecca Moses (10)
St Teresa's RC First & Middle School, Harrow Weald

My Family

My mum is like my diary, I tell her everything.
My brother, well, what can I say, he's like a tiger catching his prey.
My dad, I love him to bits, but sometimes he can be a bit of a witch!
My cat, he rules the roost, to give us all a very big boost.

Jasmine O'Neill (11)
St Teresa's RC First & Middle School, Harrow Weald

Number Mania!

1 for history
2 for tests
3 for SATs
Oh, can I have a rest?

4 for assemblies
5 for school
6 for friends
Who are so cool!

7 for homework
8 for pens
9 for sticky tape
The list never ends!

Now you have heard all about school
Can you keep a secret . . . ?
It rules!

Zoë Mendez (11)
St Teresa's RC First & Middle School, Harrow Weald

Holiday By The Sea

I love my holidays by the sea,
My mum and dad, my brother and me.

We play volleyball on the sand,
Hitting the ball and wondering where it will land.

Staying in beautiful hotels, my favourite is the shape of a sail,
To see the strobe lighting running up and down like a whale.

On a desert safari, surfing the sand dunes,
Back in Wild Wadi, zooming down the water flumes.

Alex Sheridan   (10)
St Teresa's RC First & Middle School, Harrow Weald

I Wish I Was . . .

I wish I was a frog,
So I could hop around, around,
I wish I was a dog,
So I could make a barking sound.

I wish I was a butterfly,
So I could flutter far and wide,
I wish I was a fox, so sly,
So I don't have to run and hide.

I wish I was a slimy snake,
So I could squeeze you really tight,
Or a hippo in the lake,
But watch out mate, I bite.

But all this doesn't worry me,
'Cause I don't want to get some fleas.

I just wish that I was me,
So I can make my own green tea!

Andrew Gibbs (11)
St Teresa's RC First & Middle School, Harrow Weald

My Fish!

I had a fish
Who lived in a dish
His name was Goldy
He was mouldy.

I went away
And I came back yesterday
Goldy wasn't mouldy
He was foldy (backwards and forwards).

My dad had not fed him
Which led him to death
My dad had flushed him down the loo
Because he didn't know what to do.

Kathleen McGoldrick (11)
St Teresa's RC First & Middle School, Harrow Weald

St Joe's Football Club

St Joe's are the best
Better than the rest
Looking after Rob
Who eats far too much grub.

Rob looks after us every day
Giving us matches on Saturday.

Training on Monday
Keeping really fit
Eating and drinking
6.00 to 7.00.

I played on Saturday
And I got kicked in the ankle
And went off till half-time.

I scored two goals
And Shannen scored one,
So we don't know
Who's the girl of the match.

Lauren Callaghan (10)
St Teresa's RC First & Middle School, Harrow Weald

My Best Friend

My best friend is fast like a cheetah,
My best friend is loud like a lion,
My best friend is mad like a monkey,
My best friend is funny like a chimpanzee,
My best friend is annoying (sometimes) like a puppy,
But none of these things add up to how much I like my best friend!

Gemma Evans O'Connell (10)
St Teresa's RC First & Middle School, Harrow Weald

Hurricane

Shut the windows
Bolt the doors
Look what's coming
It's scary like the dark
Big like the wind
Crashing through the street
Like an enormous hippopotamus
Everybody hide, it's coming our way
We're in the pitch-black
With a dinosaur on our roof
We're saying our prayers loud
Suddenly it's calm
What do we do?
We say let's hope it's gone away.

Sinead O'Keeffe (10)
St Teresa's RC First & Middle School, Harrow Weald

Roller Coaster

Zoom, zoom
Flying in the wind,
Twisting and turning,
As I take people on their flight.
I slowly reach to the top,
I do the loop-the-loop
As I reach my end.
Vroom! Whoosh! Cling! Clang!
Speeding down the rails,
As I laugh giving passengers *doom!*
I watch them scream as their stomach drops.
I think I'm getting too old for this job as a
Roller coaster!

Niall Foxe (11)
St Teresa's RC First & Middle School, Harrow Weald

My Little Sister And Her Book!

My darling little sister,
Loves a great book.
But one day she got angry
And decided to become a sook.

She couldn't read her book,
So she threw it really high.
She wasn't able to reach it,
So she started to cry.

My mother was not pleased,
She sent my sister to her room.
She went to get my sister's book
And tripped over the broom.

I started laughing really, really hard,
As Mum went flying across the hall.
She slammed into the door
And knocked down all my brother's balls!

She turned on me then
And shouted, 'Go to your room.'
As I stomped up the stairs,
Mum turned round and tripped over the broom!

Jessica Williams (11)
St Teresa's RC First & Middle School, Harrow Weald

Miss McCaw

Miss McCaw is 104,
In the class she always roars.
Every day she keeps us in,
I don't know why she always wins.

She has a friend called Mr Crane,
She meets him in the sun or rain.
Why, oh why, does she pick on me?
I think she needs a cup of tea!

Rafaella Notarianni (10)
St Teresa's RC First & Middle School, Harrow Weald

What And Who Are Kids?

Some kids are super cool
Some kids are fat and tall
Some kids are short and small.

Some kids are well-behaved
Some kids are white
Some kids are black
Some kids are polite.

Some kids are fun
Some kids are horrid
Some kids will make you run!

What are kids?
Kids are the people that do as they're told
But some kids are terribly bold.

Some kids have respect
Some kids have manners
I don't know, what do you expect?
Kids are kids!

Ann-Marie Hennessy (11)
St Teresa's RC First & Middle School, Harrow Weald

The Funfair

Yesterday I went to the funfair
With all the rides twisting, bobbing and flying in the air.
Eating sweets till I got sick on the floor
Till I was tucked up in bed and started to snore.

All day yesterday I had something fun to do
Even though I had to do everything with you.
I went on the rides and visited the shop
In which I bought candy and tins of pop.

When can I go back to the funfair
With the roller coaster dipping and turning in the air?

Jamie Wickham (11)
St Teresa's RC First & Middle School, Harrow Weald

Jerry The Ferret

I have a little ferret
He lingers in my bedroom
When I try to tidy up
He's always there to growl.
My finger starts to bleed
Then he sends me on a prowl.
I wait outside
And I hear a miaow.

A cat climbed in,
Stuffed Jerry in the bin,
Jerry is my ferret, I told you about him
He lives in my bedroom
And does not know how to swim.

I need to go to sleep
And I'm going to weep
So please help me
I've got to brush my teeth.

I'm over in my bed
I haven't brushed my teeth
But I can see Jerry
He's talking with Keith
The black and white cat
Who now lives with me!

Ella Ross (10)
St Teresa's RC First & Middle School, Harrow Weald

Maths

I love maths!
1+3, 2+4 and it goes along the path, I dunno.
I like subtraction, as well as a fraction,
Bar or lines, they are the same graphs to me!
Easy-peasy, easy-peasy, peasy peasy, easy-peasy,
I love maths!

Prerak Motwany (10)
St Teresa's RC First & Middle School, Harrow Weald

Messy Room

You don't have homework
You don't have anything to do
You don't have to go anywhere
You don't have to play on the PlayStation
You don't have to watch TV
You don't feel sick
You don't have to revise
You don't have to help Dad
You don't have to wash the car
You don't have to phone anyone
You don't have to help me
You don't have to listen to music
You don't have to practise football
You don't need to help your brother
You don't need to go to sleep
Just tidy your room!

Tara Ryan (10)
St Teresa's RC First & Middle School, Harrow Weald

I Dream Of . . .

I dream of playing in the sun,
I dream of having fun,
I dream there was always maths
And I dream there was always snacks.

I dream of having a cat,
I dream it's always sat on the mat,
I dreamt it slept all day like my dad
Sleeping in the hay.

Nana-Betse Parker (10)
St Teresa's RC First & Middle School, Harrow Weald

My Best Friend Ryan When He's Flying

My best friend, Ryan
Is very good at flying
He flies through the air
Just missing a bear.

He's very good at other things
But flying is his best
I just hope one day
He'll give it a rest.

Although flying sounds great
It's not when you fly into a crate
Because Ryan's oil ran out that day
And he never saw another.

Rory Carolan (10)
St Teresa's RC First & Middle School, Harrow Weald

Hurling

Hurling is an Irish sport
It simply is the best
I like the way they flick the ball
And hit it in the net.

Last year I joined a hurling club
Their name is Granuaile
I met a boy called Ryan
And he was cool as well.

Our teacher introduced hurling to the school
Ryan and I knew what to do
All our friends joined in the fun
And we won the final too.

Mark Langan (10)
St Teresa's RC First & Middle School, Harrow Weald

My Dog

My dog is fat and brown
My dog wears checked coats
My dog thinks she is a queen with a crown
My dog got lost on the boat.

My dog is lazier than a cat
My dog is slightly fluffy
My dog is content when getting fat
My dog is very fat.

My dog once ate the turkey at Christmas
My dog is quite clumsy
My dog hates jerky
My dog is clumsy.

My dog is humungous
My dog loves rice
My dog has lots of fungus
My dog is nice.

Shannen Dolan (11)
St Teresa's RC First & Middle School, Harrow Weald

Holidays

You want to have some fun,
You can play and sing in the sun.
Go to Spain in the aeroplane,
Put your swimming costume on.
Go in the swimming pool, have food and Coke,
Watch out for the mosquitoes.
There may be no Chiquita's,
No private study.
Always play with your buddy,
Now we are home again.
She is back into her study,
From now on you cannot play with your buddy!

Jasmeet Chana (10)
Springwell Junior School

The World Around Us

The tears I see, the sorrow,
I ask myself why?
The shooting, the violence,
What am I seeing with my eye?
Why does no one try to stop it?
The madness of women and men.
How can they not see what they're doing
Our world will soon end.

We should treasure
The world we have received.
Hold hands, help your neighbour,
Stop war and violence please.
A friendly smile will do,
Compliments to say
We want the world forever
Start from today.

Natasha Mudhar (11)
Springwell Junior School

Friends

My friends make me cry
When they tell me a lie.
They make me laugh
When the world is apart.
I can ask them anything I want
They never say they can't.
There are things we share,
No one else will know
We won't tell or show!

Bhavjeet Kaur Badesha (11)
Springwell Junior School

Puppy Power

Dogs will stand by you day by day,
They'll make you happy in every way,
You won't feel sad in any way,
It'll make bad cats go away,
Basketball is its favourite game.

Your dog is man's best friend,
It's sweet in every way,
Bad days won't break its pride,
Pedigree is its favourite food every day,
So keep it chubby day by day.

The best thing about a dog is everything,
There's no bad thing about a dog,
Revere its greatest deed,
Dogs are born with pure loyalty,
Dogs will be your eternal friends.

Akash Bhalla (11)
Springwell Junior School

It Must Stop!

It happens every time
It happens every day
Me gettin' punched that's all
It happens after school
Punchin', kickin', punchin', kickin'
We could go on forever
It sometimes gets really annoyin'
Just because I'm small
Nearly broke my thumb
Nearly broke my hand
It goes on and on
Phew, when will it stop?
It had better stop *soon!*

Aqib Sheikh (9)
Springwell Junior School

The Holocaust

The Nazis grab out to people with the temper
And chuck them into gas chambers.
All of the helpless families cry out in tears,
They don't have any food to eat
Which they can't bear.

More and more people are taken
Families are torn apart
And lose each other.

Each year hundreds of people die
But how many times can we find out why?
Unfortunate people are left hanging in sorrow
Will they live till tomorrow?

Children are not to learn,
Parents are not to earn,
Separated in concentration camps
Never brought back together
They all lose their hopes and gather fear.

There is now a war
Who will win?
Who will lose?
We don't know until it ends.

Finally the Jews have won
And the Nazis have been defeated!
Everyone is set free
Children can learn
Parents can earn
Let's just hope it won't happen again
And make the world a safer place.

Reema Kaur Uppal (11)
Springwell Junior School

Leave Me Alone

Leave me alone
You're not on the throne
With your big face
Don't make fun out of my race.
Whether I'm black, brown or white
You don't need to start a fight.
Don't be so cruel
'Cause you think you're so cool.
I always cry
I always sigh
I always feel like I want to die.
I hide here, I hide there
But you just simply find me everywhere
Have a heart
And change your tone,
Just leave me alone!

Davan Rayat (10)
Springwell Junior School

My Feelings

Here I stand bullied, cold
I'm stupid, dumb, that's all I'm told.

Day after day they achieve their goal
Making me a useless, empty soul.

They treat me like a piece of dirt
As I lie on the floor, tortured and hurt.

And as I look at this horrid land
Out reaches a friendly, caring hand.

A chance to play, to laugh and share
With someone who will always care.

Aleena Baig (10)
Springwell Junior School

Lonely

Here I stand, lonely and ignored,
Nobody coming up to me,
Nobody talking to me,
Everyone is happy except for me,
Everyone is playing except for me,
Everyone is picked except for me,
Why does this only happen to me?
Is it because I am different?
Or is it because I am white?
I don't know why
But why only me?
At last somebody's coming my way
I wish he would come to be my friend,
Maybe luck has come my way?

Humzah Baig (10)
Springwell Junior School

Different

I stand here isolated
I stand here hated
I just want to be respected, but I'm rejected.
I'm here all alone
No friends, just me on my own.
I'm so miserable
I feel invisible, my identity lost.
Last picked for everything
First to be picked on.
I wish I was accepted, but I'm not
I wish I had a friend, but I don't
All because I'm different.

Afiya Romain-Bains (10)
Springwell Junior School

Here I Stand

Here I stand, all alone,
Left out, somebody's nicked my phone.
At school I'm treated like dirt
Inside I'm hurt.
Here I stand, all alone,
Not accepted, violated
Here I stand, rejected, isolated
Here I stand left alone, unknown
At school I feel excluded
At school I feel stupid
I'm not accepted
I'm being bullied, bullies being racist
Nowhere to go
I'm feeling so low
I'm so emotional, so lifeless
That my body won't go
I'm feeling so left out
There's no doubt
Nobody's giving me a hand
I don't understand!

Miriam Munawar (9)
Springwell Junior School

Bullying Poem

Here I stand all alone,
Treated like dirt, like I'm unknown.
I feel left out, numb to the bone,
All my feelings are gone and I'm alone.
I feel rejected and left out
I'm useless and there's no doubt
Nobody's giving me a hand,
So I don't understand
I'm cold like a stone
And just want to go home.

Kiran Sehra (9)
Springwell Junior School

Being Bullied

I feel left out
I feel I'm the one who stands out
I feel bored and miserable at playtimes
I feel hurt at home times
I'm scared in the mornings
I have nightmares at night
I'm annoyed in class
And at lunchtimes I've nothing to eat
Because I'm the only one being bullied.

Ranjeet Nanrah (10)
Springwell Junior School

Fear

It's creeping, causing great distress,
Anxiety sets in as it draws closer,
Making the situation extremely uncomfortable,
Screaming may take away the eerie feeling.

Tara Dogra (10)
Springwell Junior School

At School

I was in school where people are cruel
After school when the bell rang
I took a book called *White Fang*
A boy tricked then he kicked
And then I never went back to school again.

Faisal Qureshi (10)
Springwell Junior School

No More Bullying

Every day they kept punchin' and kickin'
In lesson time they started pinchin'
I want it to stop!
Then one day I blew my top!
I looked at the bullies agitated
One of them actually fainted
Because I was small
And they were tall
I was not bullied again.

Zak Zaheed (9)
Springwell Junior School

All About Me!

I am always miserable and annoyed
I am feeling left out, annoyed and ashamed
I am lonely and you just make me groany.
It is very unfair, all you do is go to the funfair
It is very hot because of the sun
And you are having lots of fun, I'm not dumb!

Nikkita Tilwani (9)
Springwell Junior School

I Am A . . .

I am frightened, annoyed
Sad, I'm uncomfortable
Lonely, I'm alone
I'm scared -
I'm a prisoner.

Shahaan Malik (10)
Springwell Junior School

Why Jews?

I don't know why I feel so small
Everyone treats me like a tiny ball.
School is finished, I cry so much
And someone just took my lunch.
'Oi you, give it back! That's not fair!'
'Do you really think I care?'
I yell, I yell
I stick up for myself
Then the cruel boy replied with a smack on my face
Why me? Why us?
I hate myself, I hate my school
All I want is to be treated the same
But all the time I get the *blame!*

Binisha Shah (10)
Springwell Junior School

Here I Stand

Here I stand alone, trying not to cry
I feel left out, picked on, not to be made
I want to die, that's how I feel
They have stolen my pride, my joy and my heart!
Inside I feel cold, lonely
I just need a friend to help me through this problem
I want to cry, but I have to be strong
The words they call me, pain and repeat in my heart.
Here they come, something in store for *me* today,
Maybe a punch, maybe a kick, but whatever, it's going to hurt.
There is something they don't know that I know,
It's *friendship,* that's what I need!

Navina Kaur Bagri (9)
Springwell Junior School

It's Not My Fault!

It's not my fault, I'm black,
It's not my fault, I'm white,
It's not my fault whatever colour I am.

It's not my fault, who I am,
It's not my fault, who you are,
So, you big bully leave me alone,
You make me shiver to my bone.

You hide my property or steal what I have bought,
One day, red-handed, you'll get caught.

I've tears rolling down my cheek,
Oh I forgot you do *not* care,
So why should I tell you how I feel?
This isn't fair!

People come up to me and ask me
'How do you do?'
I reply, 'Fine,'
What can I do?
But deep down in my heart,
I'm feeling the pain that you have caused.

So for the last time,
Bully, *it's not my fault*
So leave me alone!

Sobia Rahman (10)
Springwell Junior School

Football

Fire, as Beckham kicked the ball,
The ball was flying in the air,
It rebounded off the crossbar,
Then Paul Scholes kicked it in the goal,
There was only one place for the ball to go,
It was the back of the net,
The goalkeeper hangs his head in shame.

Harjot Samra (10)
Springwell Junior School

Playground Poem

We eat at lunch,
We eat and munch,
I'm eating a bun
Let's eat while we run.

We'll whisper and we'll shout,
We'll let you know when we're about,
We will smile and cry,
As each day goes by.

It's raining! It's raining!
Oh what a pain,
Hey
Now comes the sun,
Let's all play,
This will be fun.

Look! There goes the whistle,
It's time to go,
Let's stand in a row.

Reetika Kamboh (9)
Springwell Junior School

Playground Poem

Children are playing,
Running and shouting,
Teachers looking for
Anything that's happening.
Activities to play
Fun or boring,
Doesn't really matter,
Children chatter.
The whistle has blown
Children line up,
There is hush in the playground,
I look back to see how much I have grown.

Renuka Varma (9)
Springwell Junior School

Go Away!

My eyes are waterin'
As tears are fallin'
You've left me strugglin'
You're just bullyin'
I just want to do somethin'
No use tellin'
What will I be gettin'?
My heart is breakin'
As my scabs are peelin'
I've got non-stop bleedin'
I try runnin'
But my feet keep tremblin'
Each step I'm takin'
My bruises are hurtin'
No use escapin'
Fear of dyin'
I want to share my feelin'
Although no one's carin'
Anger is comin'
Sweat is appearin'
My heart can feel it but my mouth can't say it, *go away!*

Shreena Acharya (9)
Springwell Junior School

Children, Children

Children are playing all around the playground,
They are shouting and excited with friends,
Sounds of laughter and chatting loudly
Is heard all over the playground,
Children are hiding and seeking in the playground.

Qasim Hassan (8)
Springwell Junior School

Why Do I Get Bullied?

Leave me alone,
I want to go home
Stop bullying me,
Why is it me?
When I go to school
Kids start stealing things off me,
When I walk to my house,
People call me names,
All I want is to be left alone,
Why do they bully me?
I feel like running to my mummy,
I get tears falling down me,
Why is it me? Why? Why? Why?
Is it because I am weak or I'm a wimp?
Why do they bully me? Will they stop bullying me?
I wonder, why do they bully me?

Jaymin Raja (10)
Springwell Junior School

Go Away!

Fast chasin'
Me runnin'
Gas poisonin'
German bullin'
Powerful whippin'
People dyin'
I am shoutin'
Eatin' nothin'
My skeleton breakin'
Try ignorin'
Bombs firin'
People cryin'
Hearts breakin'
Hand not movin'
Will I be here tomorrow?

Parmveer Dhami (10)
Springwell Junior School

What Have You To Prove?

Every day, lunch and play, I'm too scared to say
I try to ignore, they do some more
As I'm bullied,
I hold back a tear in spite of my fear,
Rejected, dejected, is how I feel,
Making your fantasy for real,
Doing your dirty work, man you're just a criminal,
You're making us unadditional,
My heart is saying,
But my mouth is hiding the truth from you,
What have you to prove?
You aren't cool,
You're a fool,
You pick on people younger than you,
You take my dinner money away but you just wouldn't say,
I have no one to talk to but to pray, pray, pray.

Yayra Frantzen (9)
Springwell Junior School

Who Do You Think You Are?

Keep your fist away,
Can't you use it another day?
I feel so small,
But you're so tall,
What have I done to you
And who is going to tell me what to do?
You're not on the throne,
So why don't you just leave me alone?
I feel like a slave,
But I have not yet been saved,
I have got a solution,
Go away you fool,
You wouldn't be cool,
Now I told Miss,
Who do you think you are?

Mansoor Aman (9)
Springwell Junior School

The Nazi Soldier

I feel like I am lonely,
I feel like I am sad,
I came back from school,
And one night, I saw a Nazi soldier,
I ran and ran but he caught me,
Slapped me and threw me on the ground,
He said to me, 'What are you doing?'
I said, 'Going to the theatre,'
Then he slapped me and threw
Me on the ground again!

Amandeep Chauhan (9)
Springwell Junior School

The Boy Who Wanted To Be An Adult

Everyone else is outside,
But no not me, I'm under the thumb,
Miserable and lonely, no one likes me,
Cares about me. Anxious to get attention,
It is like a jailhouse.
Now the teacher shouts at me.

Syed Aadil Ali (9)
Springwell Junior School

I Always Get Picked On

I always get picked on,
But I always get nicked,
I am so lonely and everyone
Thinks I'm so moany,
I like to play and I like to do displays,
I'm feeling let down and everyone
Calls me a clown.

Chelsea Bailey (10)
Springwell Junior School

Guess Who I Am?

I floated lonely over the hills,
Which stay stuck firm on the ground,
Being pushed and shoved,
By the wind,
Flying round and round,
Past the busy workplaces,
Traffic, road works too.
Doctors and nurses helping the sick,
I'm wisping in the sky,
So blue.
From the extra turbulent city,
To the tranquil countryside,
On the howling, revolving
And spiralling wind,
I love to ride.
The farms are extra busy,
With horses, sheep and cows,
Pigs and quite a few Billy goats
Are wandering outside the house.
I wish I could see my siblings again,
Family members too,
I wonder what they are doing right now
If only I just knew,
I'm going to ask you a question,
and tell me if you know
Just exactly what I am?

I'm a dandelion!

Jessica Esposito (11)
Springwell Junior School

I Wish People Would Notice Me

There they stand bullying me,
Laughing and joking,
I feel heartbroken,
Mum told me I'll
Make new friends, but
I think she is wrong.
I feel unhappy and alone,
They destroyed my doll,
It was my only friend,
Everyone calls me stupid.
Everyone is ignoring me,
I feel like dust just
Flowing through the air
Helpless and lifeless,
PS: Can someone just accept me!

Kayleigh Igoe (10)
Springwell Junior School

All Alone In This Big World

Here I lay on the ground,
They beat me up like a hound,
I've just been violated,
Always isolated.
I will still pray,
But why do I still lay?
I miss my snug warm bed,
My favourite colour, it was red.
Why are the bullies so, so, crazy?
How can they say that I am lazy?
Everyone looks at me, I feel absurd,
I wish I could be set free and fly like a bird.

Ilisha Haizel (9)
Springwell Junior School

Snowman

Floating dreamily,
The white old lady,
The candyfloss in a child's hand.
Melting softly in her mouth,
Trickling down the throat,
It is icy-cold,
The sun its enemy,
Melting it, more and more,
It's crying tears of sorrow,
Friendless and lonely,
As the fight goes on,
Between the sun and snowman.
The sun takes out his sword
And slashes the snowman,
With a beam of light,
Down falls the snowman,
There is no more snowman left,
But icy-cold snow.

Narin Saad (10)
Springwell Junior School

Fairground

F unky rides, zooming fast,
A ir balloons take off like rockets,
 I ce cream cold, but tasty,
R oller coasters twisting like spaghetti,
G obble up delicious treats,
R ides that go round and round,
O h gosh, I have to pound up and down,
U nknown rides not to have a go,
N oise especially from the children,
D angerous rides not for me,
     We have so much fun at the fairground.

Tej Samra (9)
Springwell Junior School

Theme Park

I can see,
A fast crazy roller coaster and people crying
Because they just got out of a haunted house,
I can hear,
The children screaming on a frightening water ride,
And adults shouting at their children because the children
Want to go on scary rides.
I can smell,
Sizzling hot dogs and soft candyfloss,
I can taste,
Delicious doughnuts, hot chips and a tasty can of coke,
Especially coke,
That is how it is in the theme park.

Zennub Lodhi (9)
Springwell Junior School

Bluesday

Every Tuesday it's always Bluesday,
I'm always feeling blue,
I'm feeling sad and other kids
Are always feeling glad.

I feel gloomy and under the weather,
And I just don't know what to do,
I'm sick of school, they're always cruel,
They just treat me like a speck of dust,
And there's no one I can trust.

I'm tired and I'm going home,
All on my own,
I don't like Tuesday because
It's always Bluesday.

Jasmin Dhamrait (9)
Springwell Junior School

Fairground

F unky fun,
A mazing acrobats,
I nteresting ice creams,
R ound roller coasters,
G ot to get moving,
R umbling tummies,
O riginal fairground,
U mbrellas up,
N aughty rain is here,
D unking doughnuts pick up on the way.

Tania Kaur Nizzar (8)
Springwell Junior School

Winter, Winter

Winter, winter drawing near,
It's just like the Arctic full of fear,
It gives you frostbite, oh dear,
It stings like a bee,
It's attached to you,
Get off my back winter,
Where's the sun?
It's not coming back for another three months.

Inderpreet Gill (10)
Springwell Junior School

Paper

Paper gets stabbed with pens and pencils,
Gets smudged with dirty rubbers,
Paper gets ripped and torn apart,
Just because no one cares.

Paper comes in many guises,
Many shapes and many sizes.

Shayna Gandhi (10)
Springwell Junior School

My Friend

My friend is cool,
She really loves school.

My friend is kind,
She's got a great mind.

My friend is great,
She is never late.

My friend is polite,
She never gets into a fight.

My friend is helpful,
She's also very cheerful.

My friend is fair,
She will always care.

My friend is cool,
She really loves school.

Sasha Raj Dorai (11)
Springwell Junior School

The Troll

Be wary of the scary monster
Who might even be a troll.

He lives in a spooky den
His blood is blue and cold.

He blobs out dirty goo
And frightens you with a *boo*.

He'll roast you on his fire
And eat you with desire.

So watch yourself when you next go
Upon your peaceful stroll.

Or you may just end up
As supper for the troll.

Baldeep Ghatore (11)
Springwell Junior School

Snow

It turns and spins in the air,
As he goes throwing icy, cold glitter.

It howls around the corners,
Leaving sugar on the way.

It bites children on their backs,
Their faces go all bright red.

Our fingers and feet glow like a shining star,

Someone's painted our windows all glimmering white,

Its beautiful, white blanket spreads gracefully everywhere it goes,

With its bad temper,
It makes all the trees bare.

With its chilly body it skips around my house magnificently

The glitter tears start to stop
The patterns on the window start to fade away,
The icy sugar starts to disappear.

He stops howling in my ear and starts to whisper instead
I think he has run away.

Inderpal Toor (10)
Springwell Junior School

Football

Charging down the pitch,
Defoe dribbles the ball,
Passes the ball to Keane,
Lobs the ball to Defoe,
Defoe sets up Kanoute,
Crosses it to Defoe,
Volleys it into the top corner like a bullet from a gun.

Marc Weir (10)
Springwell Junior School

Love

It stretches far and near,
Emptying its basket, showering us with joy.

It twirls around us,
Surrounding us, speaking from
Someone else's heart.

It dances gracefully,
Going from town to town,
Bringing warmth and happiness into their lives.

It brings your true self to light,
And polishes our future, making it gleam.

It is an exciting feeling,
Which makes us shy and light-hearted.

It should be cherished,
And not let go of, even when it demands
To be set free.

Luckveer Singh (11)
Springwell Junior School

Fire

First it starts with a little blaze,
Then bursts into action,
It creeps and crawls,
Down the hallway,
It slides under the door,
Into the room,
Then jumps on the books,
Leaving its mist of smoke,
The fire burns through the house,
Books, papers screaming in pain,
The fire does not care who it burns,
It just wants to burn!

Arron Sohota (11)
Springwell Junior School

Vicious Wind

Wind blows your cheek,
Making it red and sore.

Wind whispers secrets in my ear,
Telling me strange things.

Wind weaves its way out of the trees,
Dancing with the branches.

Wind blows your hat off,
Blowing your hair.

Wind gets vicious and howls madly.

Wind pulls the branches off the trees,
Leaving it bare.

Wind knocks the chimneys off the little houses.

Wind lifts sea, shakes it all about until frothy.

Diksha Vadhera (10)
Springwell Junior School

My Soul

My soul, it covers me with
Darkness when I'm sad.
It sprinkles light onto me
When I'm happy.
It becomes brave when
I'm embarrassed.
It becomes embarrassed when
I feel brave.
It's proud of me when
I'm ashamed of myself.
It's ashamed of me when
I'm proud of myself.
My soul is my inside ghost
Not my inside self.

Ajmeer Giasey (10)
Springwell Junior School

Diary

I'm plain and white,
I hold no words,
Only the ones you give me,
I only reflect the words you write,
Most of the time I lie under your pillow,
Sleeping until you awake me,
And fill me with your thoughts.

I am what lies within you,
I am your mind,
I have waited so long,
I am starting to get lonely,
I await under your pillow,
To be filled with more of your thoughts,
The unspoken words of . . .
Your soul.

Natasha Younus (10)
Springwell Junior School

Danger In The Playground

Children are running in the car park,
Bullies are bullying, pushing and hitting,
Teachers are shouting and telling off,
Children are yelling in the quiet area screaming and running,
Tinies are crying and whinging,
Boys are cheating and fouling,
Girls are whispering and fighting,
Children are squirting their drinks,
But I am just sitting, sitting there watching.

Puja Sharma (9)
Springwell Junior School

Feeling Different

I feel sick,
They call me thick,
I have a son,
They show me a gun.

I have no home,
Like a gnome,
I have no fun,
Like a bun.

They show me a knife,
I don't have a life,
I have to take a pill,
Now I'm going for the kill.

I have no one with me,
No one understands me.

Akshay Manro (10)
Springwell Junior School

I Feel Like A Victim

I was let down and annoyed,
I felt left out and lonely,
I was frightened and alone,
I started feeling blue,
I felt different,
I felt sad,
I felt scared,
I felt bored,
I was anxious,
I was angry,
I was miserable,
I was worried,
I was upset,
I was gloomy,
Until the Germans set me free.

Paayal Gandhi (9)
Springwell Junior School

My Life!

I hate myself, I hate my school,
I hate the children, why are they so cruel?
They kick and punch all the time,
I feel that all I'm doing is mime, mime, mime!

I have no friends, I'm all alone,
All I've got is one little phone,
I'm feeling blue, I'm feeling down,
All of this because my hair is brown!

I showed them respect, *why! Why! Why!*
I just feel as if I'll *die! Die! Die!*
I don't think I can take anymore,
My back, my legs, my feet are really sore.

Why me, why the Jews?
I just hope this never happens to you!

Harleen Mangat (9)
Springwell Junior School

A Message To Be Heard!

I feel like I'm under the thumb,
Nobody cares, why should they?
I feel lonely, left out and sad and
I'm ashamed to be who I am.
I hide away from people because
I'm too scared to stand up to them.
I feel uncomfortable knowing
Something might happen to me,
Or my family,
I hide in an attic behind a bookshelf,
Worried if I am found or not.

So here's a message from Anne Frank,
Never ever give up!

Nina-Joyce Shehata (9)
Springwell Junior School

Why Me?

I was frightened,
I was scared,
Under the thumb,
Let down,
Left out,
Under the sun,
Lonely,
Miserable,
Feeling blue,
Annoyed,
I glared,
I don't know who,
Anxious,
Agitated,
I started to pray,
Sad,
Gloomy,
I lay in hay.

Manika Tamrat (9)
Springwell Junior School

The Nazi Child

I felt left out
I walked sadly onto the streets,
It is horrible,
I was lonely,
The bully punches me!
I hate the bully!
I punch the bully,
The bully doesn't come back.

Jayraj Dosanjh (8)
Springwell Junior School

Music

Hip-hop and rap,
Rock with a tap,
Opera that's smooth,
And language sometimes rude,
Shaggy with 'Wasn't me,'
Kelis with 'Trick me,'
Booming all around,
On digital surround,
Laughter and sadness,
Beautiful and madness,
Love and hate,
Divorce and fate,
Kiss and flirt,
Miss and alert,
Music is everywhere in every way,
Just listen for different music day by day.

Somya Sharma (11)
Springwell Junior School

Go Away

G o away, leave me alone,
O h, get out of my sight and never come back!

A ll I want is you to *vanish*!
W eeping and crying you punch me all the way,
A ll I want is you to *leave*!
Y do you punch, kick me?
    Can you just live in a world of peace?

Haaris Ilyas (9)
Springwell Junior School

The Tree Was Bullied

The tree gets bullied,
Children break his arms,
The wind pushes him back and forth,
His only friend is rain, rain feeds him,
Leave the tree alone,

The tree gets bullied,
Cats jump on him,
Grass surrounds him,
Autumn takes his leaves,
Leave the tree alone.

The tree gets bullied,
People climb him,
Lightning hits him,
Some people cut him,
Leave the tree alone.

Edward Murphy (10)
Springwell Junior School

Fairground

F rightening red roller coaster,
A mazing tides flying around,
I ce cream dripping everywhere,
R ound and round the rides go,
G alloping round on horses,
R oller coasters flying and shouting,
O ld people trying to walk,
U ncaring people hitting old people,
N eighbours shouting louder and louder,
D angerous rides.

Sukhraj Randhawa (8)
Springwell Junior School

My Miserable Life

Here I stand, cold and alone,
I feel restless and just like an ice cube,
There they stand picking on people,
Like me being picked on and unhappy,
They're stupid and cruel and rejecting me,
Year 6 girls and boys can be hurtful to me and my friends,
It's like I'm being treated like dirt,
I'm miserable and sad and being tortured like mad,
They're excluding me, and I'm left out,
It's like there is something they know
That I don't know about,
Are they gonna steal something precious from me?

Tanishar Kaur Brar (9)
Springwell Junior School

Bullying

Here I stand all alone,
Angry and sad,
They've stolen everything,
Leaving me hurtful and bad.

They make me feel useless,
They make me feel like dirt,
Every single day,
Pulling my shirt.

Everybody's ignoring me,
I feel so rejected,
They make me feel so stupid,
And I'm never the one who's selected!

Duha Mohamed (10)
Springwell Junior School

Feelings

Here I stand all alone in the cold,
No one wants to be my friend,
Everyone treats me like dirt,
They think that I am invisible and ignore me,
They think I am stupid and isolated,
But then I thought I'm tough too and
Decided to go and tell him to leave me alone,
But he punched me on the floor,
There I lay on the floor,
But a hand of friendship pulled me up
He said, 'Are you alright?' and I said, 'I'm fine.'
The bully came back again but a friend saved me,
The bully never comes back again.

Divya Sareen (9)
Springwell Junior School

Why Me?

I'm the one who doesn't know how to be cool,
I'm the one known as a fool.

He's the one who wished he was dead,
He's the one ignored like a loaf of bread.

Here's the dark coming to me,
I'm just longing to break his knee.

Here I am finding a friend,
Just hoping my life would come to an end.

This is the person who really cares and
I will share my every fear.

Aman Ubhi (10)
Springwell Junior School

Fairgrounds Are Fantastic

F is for fabulous food smelling delicious,
A is for the breezy air blowing on your face,
I is for the incredible rides doing loop-the-loop,
R is for the roller coasters going really fast,
G is for the generous security guards taking you to your mums,
R is for the rough rides bashing in the dodgems,
O is for the juicy oranges in the food stores,
U nder and over the roller coasters go whooshing past your face,
N is for the naughty children running like mad,
D is for the dirty grounds blowing in the wind.

Amaris Lakhe (9)
Springwell Junior School

Here I Stand

Here I stand all alone,
I feel like they want to break a bone.
I feel invisible like a gnome.
I feel violated like a stone,
Everybody hates me, they are going to isolate me,
Everybody thinks I'm useless,
But there is a person inside me begging for respect.

Steffan Green (10)
Springwell Junior School

My Feelings

Here I stand crying,
Feeling very sad and standing all alone,
I feel left out and excluded,
I'm miserable and everyone ignores me,
People treat me like dirt, no one plays with me,
But I wish someone would!

Rick Kular (10)
Springwell Junior School

Dreams

As I lay in my bed
My tiredness flowing to my head

All wrapped up comfortable and warm
A kiss planted on my cheek
Now I am feeling all snug
A journey in a dream is what I seek.

My brain takes me to another land
Where everything is all beautiful and grand

It's an enchanted place, shiny and bright

Jewels glimmering across the land
Fairies skipping happily hand in hand.

Faeza Butt (11)
Springwell Junior School

Here I Stand

Here I stand waiting to go home,
There he stands watching me,
The bell rings, run home.
The bully is following me,
I slip then I get back up,
The bully pushes me and
My bag goes into a big puddle.
Scared I say, 'I will get you,' and run home,
I try to sleep, but I can't.
Next morning I get back up,
We had scared the bully straight away,
That's my story about me and the bully.

Rishi Dhokia (9)
Springwell Junior School

Funky Fair

Go to the fair and swing in the air
Something's begun so have fun
Have a smile for a while
Because when you enter the ghost train you'll faint.

Go to play, have a good day
The fair is cool, the food makes you drool
Prizes to win, win a fish with a golden fin
Roller coasters everywhere, a lovely time at the fair.

Drinks and food like lemonade, people calling, 'Get your Lucozade'
Whirly rides, curly rides
Colours, colours everywhere, candyfloss, lots to spare
Hot dogs and ice cream everywhere.

Fun, fun everywhere, I've got some time to spare
Let's enjoy the rides today and I'll invite you to play
So let's have fun while I have begun
Wet rides with bubbling foam, now it's time to go home.

Amrit Ghatore (8)
Springwell Junior School

Theme Parks

I love theme parks,
I always stay until it's dark,
Candyfloss is all I like,
Even though I love kites,
People think I'm really crazy,
Even though I'm really lazy,
All the rides are really fun,
I wish I had one more day,
To go to the theme park and play.

Sonam Dhani (9)
Springwell Junior School

What It's Like To Be Bullied!

You think you're so cool,
But you're a fool.
Don't bully me,
I'm innocent,
Can't you see?
Don't use that tone,
Leave me alone.
If you use your fist,
I'll tell Miss.
Don't touch me,
Or I'll climb the tree.
It doesn't matter if you're a Christian, or a Jew,
A Muslim or a Hindu,
Try not to start a fight,
Keep your anger in,
Or put it in the bin.
I try walking away,
But my feet are stuck with clay.
I just want to stay home,
And be alone.

Aaron Uraon (9)
Springwell Junior School

Funky Fairground

Come to the fairground, it is a lot of fun,
People screaming on the roller coasters,
People dreaming on the roundabout,
People dodging and bumping into each other,
Dodgems, what fun the fairground is,
All the sweets you can eat,
All that candyfloss all pink and fluffy,
What a mess you can make,
All the rides going up and down,
What fun the fairground is.

Jaspreet Gill (9)
Springwell Junior School

You Made Me Sad

I thought I had friends,
But then you changed,
All of a sudden you made me sad,
The dirty looks,
The nasty remarks,
Not wanting me near,
You knew I could hear,
I didn't want to go to school,
I couldn't learn,
I felt a fool,
You made me cry,
You didn't care why,
You left me out,
I wanted to shout,
I felt alone,
All on my own,
I was confused,
You seemed amused,
But I was strong,
And you were wrong,
In the end,
I made new friends.

Rachael De Conto (10)
Springwell Junior School

What Is Blue?

Blue is the sea shining in the light,
Blue is feeling sad when you're down in the dumps,
Blue is a whale, biggest in the world,
Blue is a snowflake lightly floating,
Blue is coldness you feel inside, when you feel alone,
Blue's the colour that stands out most,
Blue is sensitive and your friend, no doubt about it,
But can you imagine living life without it?

Javneet Malhi (11)
Springwell Junior School

Leave Me Alone

Leave me alone
You're not on the throne
When I first saw you I thought
You were really nice.
But I found out you were a bully
Now I'm terrified.
I sat with you at lunchtime
You kicked me on the leg
What do you want me to do?
Please don't make me beg
I joined my mum at church yesterday
It made no difference though
I'm really scared, I'm really tired
Please don't make me go
You've bruised me high, you've bruised me low
I think you've even broken my toe
I've not watched TV in three whole days
No hugs from Mum, no cuddly days
You should be grateful, I haven't told anyone
Mum asked me what was wrong
I said, 'Haven't been to school for a long time
Please don't make me go.'

Ranvir Sandhu (10)
Springwell Junior School

The Wind

The wind roars as it causes more destruction.
It breaks and hurts everything weaker and in its way.
Now it's turned angry and turned into a hurricane smashing
and demolishing everything.
Its thunderous roar scares everyone.
The people's cries grow terrifyingly louder,
but the bully cools down and goes away.

Gaurav Malhi (10)
Springwell Junior School

The Wind

Wind whistles through the air,
So silent no one knows he is there.
But then he twists and turns around,
And creates a sort of whistling sound.
Leaves rise from the ground,
Then in the air and all around.

The branches of trees move to and fro,
They hang desperately from their roots below.
Animals hide and people run,
Wind wrecks children's games and ruins their fun.
He blows away leaves and pushes down trees,
He sinks ships and moves the sea.

Now people know he's there,
Invisible amongst the air.
He can sneak through doors without the key,
But people ignore what they cannot see.
Except when wind is tired of being quiet,
And once again creates a riot.

Wind is all around us both low and high,
He can move clouds high in the sky.
Space is the only place where there is no wind or air,
Therefore no animals could ever live up there.
But down on Earth wind can even move the sea,
The mighty sea seems to do what he pleases.

Onkar Bansal (11)
Springwell Junior School

Read

Read, read, read
Reading is fun
But too old to be fun
So make sure you read
And you will have fun!

Amrita Gandhi (9)
Springwell Junior School

The Calculator

The calculator cried out in pain,
As its stomach was poked and pressed,
Its memory was going to explode,
It made an M appear on the screen signalling for mercy,
But they ignored it and carried on poking,
The calculator could not take it anymore,
It shouted out and an E appeared standing for enough, enough,
Finally it was allowed to rest,
The calculator could not stand maths.

Demi Ryan (11)
Springwell Junior School

Fairground

F antastic, funky fairground full of people
A ir rides, we like hot-air balloons
I ce cream, chocolate my favourite
R ockin' roller coaster ride
G ifts you can win from small stalls
R umbling stomachs running to the food stalls
O utside people screaming loudly
U nder your clothes, trembling with fear
N oisy children coming out of the haunted house.
D ads, mums, everyone at the fairground
S o that's the fairground, how great!

Simran Khangura (8)
Springwell Junior School

Silly Billy

Silly Billy where are you?
Silly Billy how are you?
Silly Billy what do you do?
Silly Billy what can you do?
Silly Billy are you blue?

Sukhdeep Mohain (8)
Springwell Junior School

Playground

P is for playing games like hide-and-seek, stuck in the mud
L is for laughing
A is for eating an apple
Y is for yawning when you're sleepy
G is for playing football and getting excited
R is for reading in the quiet area
O is for eating an orange
U is for taking out an umbrella
N is for loud noise, and
D is for having a refreshing drink.

Hira Bashir (8)
Springwell Junior School

Summer

I like the summer,
I like the sun,
I like it because
It's fun.

The summer is hot,
The summer is dry,
When my friends come out
We say *hi!*

Simran Patel (9)
Springwell Junior School

The Big School

Playing, playing, playing,
There's nothing to be afraid of,
Run free around the playground,
Friends, friends, you can't be without them,
Happy children, sad children,
Come and play in this wonderful playground!

Hetan Dilip Bhesania (9)
Springwell Junior School

Playground

Football crazy, happy faces,
Girls skipping with loose laces.

I play tag with Zak, Vishal and Amaris,
And I bump into Miss and she screams like a maniac,
And tells me off with a hiss.

Back in the playground, after eating my butterscotch tart,
It's time to have a race,
Zak shouts, 'Start!'

It's time to do some work, playtime is over,
This afternoon's lesson is science,
Perhaps we'll study a supernova?

Ibrahim Haizel (8)
Springwell Junior School

Bullying

There was a bully not long ago
He used to fight for a show.

He was a mean, clean fighting machine
He loved grinding people's feet.

There was a bully not long ago
He used to fight for a show.

One day it came
For his turn to fight
But the bully was right
And wished never to fight again.

Jaga Johal (9)
Springwell Junior School

The Hideous Holocaust!

The Holocaust is hideous,
mean and dreadful.
Families get separated
and loved ones die.
The Holocaust brings anger,
pain and sorrow.
At the concentration camps
people starve.
Hundreds of people in gas chambers,
dying of the gas, food and thirst,
while we are here,
all happy and joyful.
We should spare a thought
for those who are less fortunate!

Avneesh Kaur Segue (11)
Springwell Junior School

Rude Nelly

Nelly is rude,
Nelly is blue,

Nelly is sad,
Because she thinks she is bad,

Nelly does not come,
Because she is sad,

Nelly is happy,
Because she is good,

Nelly has friends,
So she will come to school every day.

Meera Kara (9)
Springwell Junior School

The Violent Wind

It roars with anger,
It whistles violently,
It bullies the trees and it also bullies me.
It scares the sea and it also scares me,
I'm afraid of it, as it may blow me away,
I can see it, I can see it, it's coming my way,
I've escaped from its arms and it's done me no harm.
It's the wind,
It's the wind.

Rumneet Johal (10)
Springwell Junior School

Playground Poem

P laytime!
L itter bin
A lways happy
Y es or no?
G ames
R unning mad
O bey people
U s 2?
N aughty?
D ancing.

Dhruv Upadhyaya (8)
Springwell Junior School

My Goldfish

My goldfish is shimmery brown,
My goldfish loves to swim around.
My goldfish eats a lot of food,
She's always in a merry mood.
My goldfish is a wonderful pet,
She's a fish I'll never forget.

Reema Patel (10)
Springwell Junior School

Leave Me Alone!

Is it my fault
That maybe I am a different colour to you?
Is it my fault?

Every day you bully me
What do you want?
Why do you do this?

My heart is beating faster than ever
I shiver and tremble
You just walk up to me
And punch me.

Why do you do this?
If you have nothing to prove
Leave me alone!

Meghana Kotipalli (9)
Springwell Junior School

Go Away Kennings

Blood pourin'
Heart achin'
Leg shakin'
Knife cuttin'
I try runnin'
But you're holdin'
I try fightin'
But it don't solve nothin'
I try screamin'
But nobody's listenin'
Why do you bully?
Cos you're just a phoney
You've left me cryin'
I try tellin'
But they think I'm lyin'.

Harkaran Thind (10)
Springwell Junior School

At The Fairground

People screaming and shouting
Looking up at the fireworks
So many different colours and different lights
Animals running here and there
Children laughing and screaming on different rides.

At the fairground I can smell . . .
Onions sizzling in the pan
Popcorn going *bang! Bang!*
Having ice cream yum, yum, yum
Eating hot dogs, filling my tum.

At the fairground I can hear . . .
Fireworks blazing in the dark blue sky
Children screaming and shouting with happiness
Animals running for safety.

Fairground fun . . .
Fairground fun . . .
Fairground fun . . .

Maira Iqbal (9)
Springwell Junior School

At The Fairground!

At the fairground I can see . . .
Children laughing everywhere
Grown-ups stop and stare

At the fairground I can hear . . .
Excited children's cheers
Grown-ups begin to relax

At the fairground I can smell . . .
Sizzling sausages all around
Grown-ups let their hair down.

Amanjot Grewal (9)
Springwell Junior School

At The Fairground

3 . . . 2 . . . 1 . . . here we go
get ready to see the circus show

Balls juggling up and down
in your hand, round and round

3 . . . 2 . . . 1 . . . here we go
get ready to see the circus show

All the food so, so nice
keeping away all the mice

3 . . . 2 . . . 1 . . . here we go
get ready to see the circus show

Come on in the haunted house
there's lots of fun
Let's follow the headless mouse

There's ice cream melting and hot dogs steaming
There's more to do, so let's keep dreaming

3 . . . 2 . . . 1 . . . here we go
get ready to see the circus show.

Yashna Abhol (9)
Springwell Junior School

Fairground

F un . . . fun . . . fun . . .
A ll around in the fairground sun
I ce cream melting on my tongue
R ides zoom up and twirl around
G host train moves without a sound
R oasted nuts, popping popcorn
O nions sizzle for the burgers
U p and down . . . the rides swoop fast
N oise . . . laughter fills the fairground
D unking donuts eaten on the merry-go-round.

Gurjyott Sehmi (8)
Springwell Junior School

Fairground

I see the roller coasters going like a bolt of lightning
and zooming down.
I see the smiles on children's faces.
I hear the children scream from the roller coaster
and the water rides.
I smell the delicious smell of the candyfloss, sizzling sausages
and the cold ice cream which goes through my mouth.
People going in and out of the fairground.
The merry-go-round makes me dizzy and some other rides too.
Fairgrounds are fun but scary too.
There are little games like the duck hooking and many others too.
The clowns are funny and I couldn't stop laughing at them.
Visit the fair and you will be happy.

Pooja Amirneni (9)
Springwell Junior School

At The Fairground

Sizzling burgers
Sticky sweets
Looping roller coasters
Bouncing off seats

Twirling, looping in the sun
Laughing, eating, having fun

Fireworks zooming
Everywhere

Scary ghost trains
Raising hair

Twirling, looping in the sun
Laughing, eating, having fun.

Simran Chana (8)
Springwell Junior School

At The Fairground

3 . . . 2 . . . 1 . . .
Are you ready to go?
Make sure you have your wallet to play *bingo!*

Balls are juggling up and down
Here comes . . .
The circus clown

The smell of the popcorn goes up my nose
You really can't resist it
It's got a better scent than a rose

The roller coaster ride looks really fast
Let's hope it doesn't break down
Or you'll end up in a cast.

The sun goes down
It's time to go home
I really will miss . . .
The circus clown.

Shivraj Aulakh (9)
Springwell Junior School

Fairground

F is for fun and frightening rides.
A is for action rides.
I is for idiots bumping into walls.
R is for rocking roller coaster.
G is for graveyard in the haunted house.
R is for rocks, hard to bite.
O is for orange juice, sweet to drink.
U is for you doing what you like.
N is for nasty surprises.
D is for doughnuts covered with sugar.

Bhupinder Dhanoa (9)
Springwell Junior School

Fairgrounds Are Fun

Fairgrounds are fun
Chefs cook yummy round buns
Roller coasters are loopy
Sausages are curly

Merry-go-rounds are round
You can hear the music sound
Games are weird
Mice are fierce
You see people having fun
Waiting for their turn to run

Haunted houses are spooky
Dirty ghosts are freaky
Crazy clowns juggle
But worms wiggle.

Jagraj Grewal (8)
Springwell Junior School

Superb Fairground

F ab fairground with groovy buns
A ncient candyfloss with chocolate buttons
I ce creams to be sold at a very low price
R umbling tummies eager to eat some food
G reat smell catches people
R oller coasters zooming up and down the funky street
O ver the dry skies rushed the kids
U nder the pirate ship lies buried treasure
N asty people waiting to get the ride of their life
   on the dragon roller coaster
D elicious candyfloss waiting to be eaten at a low price.

Vishal Bouri (9)
Springwell Junior School

The Super Theme Park

Mad things
Big things
Small things
Smelly things
Yummy things
I love everything
Do you?

Fast things
Slow things
Bad things
Good things
I think everything's amazing
Do you?

Straight things
Slimy things
Scary things
Slidy things
I love this place
Do You?

They bash and crash
They scream and shout.
I love the theme park
Do you?

The drinks are cold
The food is hot
Everything's great in this place
So let's have a cheer and maybe a beer
We've got to celebrate today
But the only problem is
When we have to go home
I hate home
Do you?

Ashanti Douglas (9)
Springwell Junior School

In My Heart

People dying
Mummy's crying
Children screaming
Gases steaming
Nazis coming
Everyone's running
Houses on fire
Trapped by barbed wire
Time of misery
I miss my family
I miss my mother
They killed my brother
Bullets everywhere
They don't really care
No time to play
A sad time all day
I feel alone
I want to go home
Too much pain
When will I see sunshine again?

Aasia Qayum (9)
Springwell Junior School

Theme Park

T he humungous roller coaster goes loop to loop
H appiness is a really fast ride
E veryone loves the acceleration
M any children screaming and laughing
E veryone loves tasty food.

P lenty of spooky and scary rides
A fterwards we had delicious toffee apples
R apidly, tasty hot dogs are made
K ind people having a fantastic day.

Jay Shinhmar (9)
Springwell Junior School

At The Fairground . . .

The rides are spinning, spinning
Peoples shouting, 'I'm winning, winning'
Eating ice cream, saying, 'Yum-yum
All the food going down my tum, tum.'

On the ride . . . twirling, twirling
Come out so dizzy . . . whirling, whirling
I'm having so much fun, fun
Shouting again, 'Come, come.'

Up the loops we go, go
Screaming at the top of our voices, 'Oh no, oh no!'
It's fun to go up and come down, down
But it makes your head go round, round.

By the corner I saw a line, line
It was the face painting time, time
It took me ages to get mine done, done
Since it took so long
The rides had started
I had to run, run.

Now the rides are closed
People have to go
When it opens again
I'll be the first to come to the show.

Divya Laxmi Sharma (8)
Springwell Junior School

Great Fairground

You see people having fun
Waiting for their turn to run
Hear people shouting, screaming
Smell food - burgers, chips, doughnuts, popcorn, very tasty
You taste burgers in a bun
Chips with ketchup - yum, yum, yum.

Lauren Chahal (8)
Springwell Junior School

At The Fairground

At the fairground I can hear . . .
Laughing clowns
Children's shouts and screams
As they queue up for ice creams

At the fairground I can see . . .
Balloons flying high in the sky
Rides zoom up so very high
Carriages, roller coasters
Children screaming

At the fairground I can smell . . .
Sizzling sausages in the frying pan
And all the baking hot dogs are the sweetest of all
Coconut shy to be won
Fill up the balloon and *pop* it goes
Lucky fish and the puppet show

Fun, fun, fun!

Manpreet Singh (9)
Springwell Junior School

Fairground Is Fun To Play

Fairground is fun to play
Children running all the way
Parents running to the haunted house
Children screaming in the dragon's house
Sausages sizzling on the grill
Children jumping and running around
Children hiding
Parents finding.

Shiza Amir (9)
Springwell Junior School

At The Fairground

At the fairground I can hear . . .
People screaming everywhere,
Sweets, candyfloss . . . yum, yum, yum,
All for me in my tum, tum, tum.

The circus clown starts his tricks,
I lick my lollipop . . . lick, lick, lick.
The tight rope walker balances on his rope,
Does he fall . . . nope, nope, nope.

The roller coaster zooms round,
It makes a lot of noise.
Clowns making funny faces,
Children eating candy laces.

At the stalls there are . . .
Burgers sizzling,
Popcorn popping,
And of course me filling my tum,
Oh yum-yum.

Aneet Gill (8)
Springwell Junior School

Theme Park

T is for the beautiful place, theme park
H is for scary haunted house
E is for exciting doughnuts, popcorn, sandwiches
    and beautiful fresh fruit
M is for mega fun
E is for excellent rides

P is for pretty looking clothes
A is for super dooper apple crumble
R is for zooming roller coasters
K is for kurly wurly slides.

Kiran Bal (8)
Springwell Junior School

Go Away

You're a big bully
You are bad
Every time I see you I faint
My legs are shaking
If you bring up your fist
I will tell Miss
You were my friend
How could you be a bully to me?
I'm sick of you
I try to scream but no one hears my cry
My heart wanted to say it
But I wouldn't dare to say it.

Gubinder Sarai (9)
Springwell Junior School

Why?

Why do you bully me?
That's the question
Why do you bully me?
With the world I'm losing connection
Why do you bully me?
I want to have friends
Why do you bully me?
You call me names every time the day ends
Why do you bully me?
I try to tell but they call me a liar
When will you ever stop?
You keep on bullying, why, why, why?

Karan Patel (9)
Springwell Junior School

At The Fairground

At the fairground I can see . . .
Everybody's faces filled with glee
I can see balloons in the sky
They are flying high up in the air
People down below watch and stare

At the fairground I hear . . .
Shouts and screams
As children wait for ice cream
Roller coaster clinks and clangs
As fireworks go off with a bang.

Zooming . . . twirling in the air
There is so much fun at the fair.

Kiranvir Gill (8)
Springwell Junior School

At The Fairground

At the fairground I can see . . .
Balls juggling up and down
Getting dizzy all around
Everybody is having fun
On the ground

At the fairground I can hear . . .
Children screaming and having fun
Licking ice cream in the glowing sun
Music blasts out loud
When I'm on the roller coaster
I feel as though I might land on a cloud

At the fairground I can smell . . .
Sizzling sausages
Popping popcorn
Dunking doughnuts all around.

Abrar Qureshi (9)
Springwell Junior School

At The Fairground

At the fairground you can see . . .
Children waiting eagerly
Hot dogs sizzling, onion rings roasting
The Ferris wheel in the clear blue sky
Stores selling
And roller coasters rising up high.

At the fairground you can hear . . .
Children screaming
Roller coaster screaming
Popcorn popping
Fireworks banging
And people shouting

At the fairground you can smell . . .
Burning popcorn
Smoking fire
Hot dogs sizzling
Lollipops
And candyfloss.

Rasib Shafi (8)
Springwell Junior School

Mohammed Ali

You can't knock him down
He's the man
He's the best
He's the king
He's the world champion
Media leave him alone
He needs a rest
Just for a day.

Zipo Mangaliso (10)
Springwell Junior School

Snow Angels

Angels fall from the sky,
Singing with a graceful voice,
Covering fields with a crisp white blanket,
Icing house cakes with a silvery tube.

Freezing lakes and rivers,
And laughing about it later,
Making children find woolly, warm clothes,
Giving presents which turn out to be colds,
Making the ground slippery so that children fall.

In the end, finally the sun comes out
And saves the day.

Manpreet Purewal (11)
Springwell Junior School

At The Fairground

At the fairground I can see . . .
Children laughing, having fun
Licking ice cream in the sizzling sun
The whole day is filled with fun.

At the fairground I can hear . . .
Fireworks banging
Engines clanging
Bumper cars crashing.

At the fairground I can smell . . .
Sticky candyfloss
Next to the ball toss
Burgers sizzle on the frying pan
Clowns made a balloon for the man.

Oh . . . don't we have fun at the fair!

Kyle Powell (8)
Springwell Junior School

At The Fairground

At the fairground I can see
Rides going up and down
Balloons being thrown in the air by a cheeky clown
Children, adults all around
Fireworks making a massive sound

At the fairground I can hear
Children screaming here and there
Music playing everywhere
Rides clink
As children blink

At the fairground I can smell
Sizzling sausages on the go
As people get ready to see the circus show
Popping popcorn
Sweet candyfloss being sold at a reasonable cost.

Darkness fills the fairground
As people go, there is not a sound.

Pawandeep Bhambra (8)
Springwell Junior School

The Book That Was Being Bullied

The book was being tortured,
While people kept slapping it,
As they turned its pages roughly.
It was getting extremely nervous,
As people kept staring at it coldly.
It screamed out in agony,
When somebody tore one of its pages.

Tanveer Bawa (10)
Springwell Junior School

Special Person

My special person is my teacher
Eyes gleaming in the stars
She loves teaching, no matter where you are

My special person is my teacher
Likes maths everywhere - maths here, maths there
Other subjects, she doesn't care.

My special person is my teacher
With her beautiful smile
It will keep your heart pumping for a while.

My special person is my teacher
Keeping 6S in line, she's doing a good job
Because she wants them all to shine.

Ritika Sharma (10)
Springwell Junior School

I Wish

I wish there was some peace in the world.
The president sitting on his chair sighing,
Trying to help by asking for money.
We're just sitting here laughing,
While other people are dying and crying across the world.

I wish the government would care for the boiling heat,
Give them water, give them food,
Give them anything to help them grow.
I wish they could grow one day a healthy life
And a home for people across the world.

I wish people
Would care.

Simran Deol (10)
Springwell Junior School

I Am

I am the washing machine
washing all the clothes,
I am the clothes
hung on the washing line,
I am the washing line
blown by the breeze,
I am the breeze
flying across the city,
I am the city full of houses,
I am the house
hearing a rumbling noise,
I am the rumbling noise
continuing my journey,
What am I?
A washing machine.

Satnam Mudhar (10)
Springwell Junior School

Fairground Fun!

F is for fabulous zooming rides.
A is for adults asking for advice.
I is for ice cream dripping and melting.
R is for rusty sausages being made in the shop.
G is for gigantic roller coasters.
R is for red noses sniffing.
O is for octopuses hanging down the string.
U is for umbrellas all over the place.
N is for nuts roasted and soft.
D is for dogs left outside.

Payal Sharma (9)
Springwell Junior School

Fairground

F is for fantastic rides zooming across the high, high skies.
A is for amazing smells in the air that go by.
I is for ice cream that you can buy at a fairground nearby.
R is for racing cars that you race and bump with.
G is for gigantic rides that you can go up then down on.
R is for roller coaster racing by.
O is for opening the door to the haunted house, scary and horrible in the dark.
U is for unbelievable things you can buy or see with your eyes.
N is for normal things, rides, food and prizes.
D is for danger and scary rides that you can find.

Onik Ahmed (9)
Springwell Junior School

Friendship

Friendship is being there for each other,
Friendship is trust.

Friendship smells of a red rose petal,
Friendship will always be there.

Friendship is when you play with each other,
And care for each other.

Friends will always be together,
Be happy and proud you have them.

Friends are hard to get,
So keep a friendship forever.

Be friends forever!

Gaganjot Panesar (11)
Springwell Junior School

Family

My family are great,
They help me when I am stuck,
They make me happy when I am sad.
Families are always there for you,
Don't ever forget that.
Your family will make you happy,
What would you do without them?
No mum, dad, brother or sister,
I could never imagine that.

Some people don't have families,
So be grateful of what you've got.
I will always be there for my family, will you?
I trust my family, do you?
Families, I wonder what yours is like?

Your family is your backbone,
They are always there for you,
No matter what.
My family are great.

Ambika Sharma (10)
Springwell Junior School

Friendship

Friendship is love for each other,
Friendship is a red, smooth petal.

Friendship smells like a delicious bowl
Of chocolate chip ice cream.

It's where we trust each other,
Play with each other,
And care for each other.

We will always be together,
No matter what happens.

Friendship is forever.

Ambhar Dar (10)
Springwell Junior School

In The Playground

In the playground playing lots of games,
In the playground talking to your friends.

In the playground screaming your head off,
In the playground picking up litter.

In the playground helping all the teachers,
In the playground having lots of fun.

Zak Rahman (9)
Springwell Junior School

Bully

My cuts are bleeding
I wish they were healing
My heart is pounding like a drum
I feel like running to my mum
They pull my hair
Like I don't care
They push
With a big whoosh
Why do they do this?

Harleen Woodwal (10)
Springwell Junior School

The Safe Classroom

The thing called a bully
A bully it is
He chases me, he taunts me
But he can't catch me or hurt me
I can run, I can hide
Into the safest place
This place is my classroom.

Drew Harry (8)
Springwell Junior School

Go Away!

My heart is breaking
You left me crying
Stop bullying or I'll bully you back
You're making me scream and my head's hurting
My skeleton is breaking
My heart is in pain
I tried telling, but I never could
Stop calling me names
Stop playing this game
I try running away, but every time I fall down.

Manvir Gill (9)
Springwell Junior School

Go Away

Go away
Oh I am very sad
I am just a little lad
Please get out of my way
I need to go to school today
I feel like crying when you are there
I am getting very scared and you don't care
My heart is bleeding
My tears are shedding
Leave me alone!

Charu Abrol (9)
Springwell Junior School